JOSEF LOCKE

THE PEOPLE'S TENOR

Nuala McAllister Hart

Croshan
Press

For Rory & Michael

He talked of English journalists who wanted to 'write his story' and offered a five figure sum of money. *"I said No. They were more interested in trivia than my showbusiness career."*

Josef Locke, in a newspaper interview in January 1971.

First Published 2017
Croshan Press

ISBN 978-1-906689-74-2

Contents

Acknowledgements

Thanks are due to:

Josef Locke's Family
Carmel McLaughlin, widow
Yvette Anderson, Karl McLaughlin and Nikki Parsons, children
Angie Cundale, niece

Fellow-performers
Roy Adams
Phil Coulter
Maureen Hegarty
William (Willie) Loughlin
Rosemary Scallon aka Dana

And
Barry Band, theatre historian, Blackpool
Martin Bradley, Derry Theatre Trust
Roma Cafolla, daughter of musician Orlando Cafolla
Maurice Colgan, Dublin
Robert Corbett, Records Manager, Belfast City Council
Frank Doran
Roy Foster, Emeritus Professor of History, University of Oxford
Irene Gunning, daughter of a 1940s RUC Officer
Brendan Hyland, nephew of Tom Daly of the Gaiety Theatre, Dublin
Barry Morris, former Director of Tourism, Blackpool
Pat MacCafferty, son of James MacCafferty
Geraldine McCallion of Drumellan House, Burnfoot, Co. Donegal (now Hegarty's B and B)
Anne McNeill, Dublin
Tom Pollock, Belfast
Mick Ryan, The Ha'Penny Bridge Inn, Dublin
The 'regulars' at Jones' Pub in Clane, Co. Kildare and Larkin's Pub in Edenderry, Co. Offaly

Acknowledgements

Finola Frawley and the staff of the Theatre Archive, Dublin City Library
Hugh Forrester of the Northern Ireland Police Museum
Dominic Kearney of the Irish Guards' Archives
Linda Ming, Heritage Officer, Central Library, Derry
Tony Sharkey and the staff of Blackpool Central Library

Nigel Johnston of Impact Printing for graphic design of the text.

And the many people I met in libraries, buses, trains, farms and elsewhere who told me their stories of Josef Locke.

But most of all to my husband and fellow-researcher, Bill Hart, who edited the text with unflagging obstinacy.

About the Author

Dr Nuala McAllister Hart is a musician and writer with a passionate interest in the history of Derry-Londonderry about which she has published widely. Her career has included university teaching, being a church organist and working for the Arts Council of Northern Ireland. Her first book *From Farquhar to Field Day: Three Centuries of Music and Theatre in Derry-Londonderry* was published by History Press (Ireland) in 2012. She now works as an arts critic, writing music and theatre reviews.

Preface

Reconstructing the story of Josef Locke's life has not been easy. There are – and always have been – myths relating to the man and his career, some of them invented or embellished by Josef (Joe) himself or his publicists. They have been picked up and recycled in newspapers and on the internet without ever having been properly checked or challenged.

There is, for example, the well-known tale of Joe's audition by Jimmy O'Dea in 1941 that launched his singing career. Did it take place in a Dublin theatre, in the Empire theatre in Belfast, or, as Joe himself once claimed, in a talent competition in a Belfast cinema? Did he, as is often repeated, top the bill in Blackpool for nineteen seasons? Did he star in five Royal Variety Performances? And what is the truth behind the notorious story of his flight from the Inland Revenue in 1958? The more closely we go back to the sources, the clearer it becomes that some parts of the myth of Josef Locke are demonstrably false, others exaggerated, and others again have acquired a rosy glow in people's memories.

The present book goes back to primary sources: contemporary newspaper reports and advertisements, theatre programmes and reviews; and weaves them together with the personal reminiscences of those who knew and performed with Joe over the years. From his early days in opera, through his heyday on the variety circuit, to his later years as the respected elder tenor.

The highs and lows in Joe's life and career were more dramatic than those of most people. He was the outstanding popular tenor of his day; but, until he came into calm waters in his mid- to later years, his private life was 'tempest-toss'd', an inexhaustible source of rumour and speculation, tame by present standards perhaps, but which became the stuff of legend.

Of course, Joe was gifted by nature with a wonderful singing voice, but what is not so well understood is how much work he put in to develop this natural talent and how much he gave of himself in his singing. This made him not just one of the most admired, and admittedly sometimes parodied, singers of his time, but one who was loved (and never forgotten) by those who heard him.

With all his flaws and contradictions, Joe just loved to sing, for the sheer pleasure of singing, and almost whether anyone was listening or not. Essentially, then, this is the story of what Josef Locke himself described as 'The Voice' – and what a remarkable voice it was.

CHAPTER ONE

A Derry Childhood 1917-1933

Birth of a Legend

At the height of his career Josef Locke sometimes claimed to have been born on 17 March, St Patrick's Day. Apt as this would have been for one of Ireland's greatest tenors, especially one known for his singing of Irish songs and ballads, it wasn't true. His birth certificate clearly gives his date of birth as Friday 23 March 1917. The son of Patrick and Annie Frances McLaughlin of 19 Creggan Street, Derry, he was christened 'Joseph' without any additional Christian name. Family and friends always called him 'Joe'.

Both Joe's parents were from Derry. They were married in the Roman Catholic Long Tower Church of St Columba, overlooking Derry's Bogside on 1 January 1902. Patrick, Joe's father, was twenty-six, his young bride six years younger. In the 1911 Census Patrick described himself as a 'flesher' – an Ulster-Scots word for butcher. His wife Annie, who came from one of the city's many Doherty families, was a machinist in a shirt factory before her marriage. Both Patrick and Annie came from large families: Patrick's father Peter McLaughlin had six children, while Annie was one of ten children of Patrick Doherty. Her father, a labourer, had already passed away at the time of her wedding.

Joe himself was the seventh of Patrick and Annie's ten children, of whom only eight survived into adulthood. Mary, the McLaughlin's first child, died at three-and-a-half years, but nine more children followed in quick succession. Annie Frances, Patrick, Thomas, Bridget [known as Bridie] and John Redmond were all born before the First World War. Joe's birth in 1917 was followed by that of Peter Brendan the following year, then Anna in 1924 and finally Richard [Dickie]. Anna was named after both her mother and her elder sister Annie, who died in 1920, when she was fifteen years old. So the McLaughlins were no strangers to infant mortality or childhood deaths. Much later, two of Joe's own children were to die in infancy.

The extended McLaughlin/Doherty family was large, and Joe would have grown up surrounded by a large tightly-knit community of aunts, uncles and cousins.

In the first few years of their marriage, the McLaughlin family lived in a terrace house in Nassau Street in the Rosemount area of Derry. It had six rooms on two floors and was built of brick with a slate roof. It fronted onto the street, with a door and single

Joe's birth certificate showing his date of birth as 23 March 1917.

window on the ground floor, and two front upstairs windows. Heating was provided by coal or peat fires in the kitchen range and the living room. By 1911 the family had moved to a slightly smaller five-roomed house in Princes Terrace, a small side street sandwiched between Clarendon Street and Great James Street. As well as the couple and their three children, Annie's brother James, a plumber, and their elderly widowed mother Elizabeth lived with them. This kind of household, with three generations living together cheek by jowl, was the norm in working-class families in Derry at this time.

Between 1911 and 1917 the family moved again, this time to 19 Creggan Street where they were living at the time of Joe's birth. The house's location, just across the road from St Eugene's Cathedral, was to prove significant for Joe's early musical education.

Joe's maternal grandmother Elizabeth Doherty – known as 'Lizzie' – was born in County Donegal around 1842. We don't know exactly when and in what circumstances she moved to Derry. Perhaps her family moved to the city to escape the Famine of the later 1840s which was felt more acutely in country districts. Perhaps they were drawn by hopes of employment in the shirt factories that from the 1850s onwards were springing up around the city. As a child Joe might well have heard stories passed down from his grandmother of her younger days in rural Donegal and had his imagination fired by them. Donegal was later to become for Joe a place he could retreat to, where he could get off his treadmill of concerts and public appearances, and enjoy the quieter pursuits of farming and golf.

Peter McLaughlin, Joe's paternal grandfather, was also born in County Donegal, in Milford. He died in May 1917, shortly after Joe was born, when the *Derry Journal* described him as a 'fervent Catholic', who 'consistently upheld the principles of Nationality during stirring times in the city'. It added that he was well-known and respected 'among the farmers and cattle-dealers of the north-west'. Peter McLaughlin had come to Derry in his teens or early twenties and in 1871 married Mary Gibbons of a city family involved in cattle-dealing. Throughout the 1870s he bid considerable sums of money to the Corporation for the right to collect the tolls for the Butter and Pork Market in Foyle Street and the City Slaughterhouse. He also had a public house at the lower end of Waterloo Street. But the death of his 26-year-old wife and two of his infant children a few months apart in 1880, was a blow from which he never fully recovered – or perhaps it just coincided with a downturn in his fortunes. We hear little of him thereafter, apart for his appearance in the 1901 Census when his occupation is given uninformatively as 'Clerk and Salesman'.

Growing up in 1920s Derry

Some of Joe's earliest memories would have been of the sectarian disturbances that preceded the partition of Ireland into the Irish Free State and the six-county Northern Ireland. On what the *Derry Journal* described as 'Derry's Night of Terror', 6-7 November 1920, Catholic-owned houses and shops in Creggan Street, where the McLaughlins lived, and in the nearby William Street were attacked, had their windows smashed and were set ablaze. That was exceptional, but sounds of gunfire and explosions in the city during the nightly curfew continued sporadically up to the end of 1923 and would have been a familiar accompaniment to Joe's boyhood.

A cattle market in Rossville Street, Derry in the 1900s where both Joe's father Patrick, and grand-father Peter McLaughlin would have done business.

Derry in the 1920s, despite its docks and shirt factories, had still something of the air of a country town. On Saturdays and market days small farmers would bring their produce – butter, buttermilk, eggs, potatoes and vegetables – into the city and sell directly from their carts. Many householders in Derry kept pigs and poultry, and even cattle in the yards behind their homes. We don't know if Joe's father was one of these, but as a butcher, he probably had some livestock of his own, looked after with his children's help.

Joe's oldest brother Patrick was ten years old when Joe was born and must have seemed almost like a man to Joe by the time he was able to take in the world around him. With three big brothers and a big sister to look after him Joe was not short of protectors in the sometimes rough world of Derry's streets and playgrounds. He was closest in age to his younger brother Brendan and there was a strong bond between them that was to last well into adulthood.

There was music in the McLaughlin family, but not of a sophisticated kind. They had a piano and Joe's mother Annie could play it, mainly the songs and popular melodies of the day that she had picked up by ear. Family members later said that that there was something 'funny' about the way she played, a reference perhaps to something individual or odd about her playing. Or perhaps she deliberately played in an amusing way?

There was music, too, in the Derry air. A journalist was later to claim that Michael O'Duffy, Patrick O'Hagan (born Patrick Sherrard) and Joe, all of whom went on to have successful international singing careers, came from the same street in Derry and sang in the same choirs. That wasn't literally true – Michael Duffy (or O'Duffy) lived in Bishop Street and Patrick Sherrard in William Street – but there does seem to have been something in the musical environment of Derry at the time that was conducive to good singing.

School and Cathedral Choirs

Joe's own introduction to singing was probably in his primary school, St. Eugene's Boys' School in Rosemount. Its Principal James Doherty (or O'Doherty) was a keen musician who regularly entered his school choir for the Boys' Choir competition at the Feis Doire Colmcille, the city's annual festival of Irish music, and conducted it himself. Under his baton St. Eugene's Boys' Choir won the competition almost every year in the 1920s. Doherty's wife Ella was herself a gifted singer and pianist and able to help in training the school choir. It may have been with St. Eugene's Boys' Choir that Joe was first heard on radio, as they sang in the Feis Prize Winners' Concert that was broadcast by the BBC in Belfast on 23 April 1927.

While at St. Eugene's Boys' School Joe was recruited to sing with St. Eugene's Cathedral Choir. The cathedral organist and choirmaster at the time was Joseph O'Brien, a member of a well-known family of church organists, music teachers and

The 'Credo' Plainsong which Joe would have sung in the Cathedral Choir.

choir-trainers in Ireland.[1] In the cathedral choir Joe would have received a grounding in sight reading and Gregorian chant as well as in a wide range of other church music. Since arriving in Derry in 1918 O'Brien had done much to raise the profile of both secular and religious music in the city and was famously enterprising and adventurous in his programming for his various choirs and orchestras.

Joe had a roguish story about his time in St. Eugene's Cathedral Choir. The principal treble Charlie McGee was a few years older than Joe, and when his voice broke, Joe was chosen to replace him. But Joe blotted his copybook in a major way when O'Brien caught him surreptitiously spitting from the choir gallery onto the bald heads of men in the pews below, and he was promptly demoted to pumping the organ.

Given that Joe was later to achieve his greatest success in variety, it is worth mentioning Derry's Opera House as a possible influence upon his early musical taste. In the 1920s it provided a varied diet of opera, concerts, pantomimes and variety shows – not to mention silent films – at prices affordable even by young boys like Joe, at a penny a time for a seat on the benches in the gallery.

Singing Solo in the Feis

It is often taken for granted that Joe must have made his mark as a boy in local singing competitions in Derry. Among these competitions the annual 'Feis Doire Colmcille' was first and foremost for Catholics in the city. But Joe never claimed to have won any prizes as a boy in the Feis. It was his older brother Patrick, and later Brendan, who were said to be the family singers. But there is a record of 'Joe McLaughlin' of St. Eugene's

---

[1] *His brother Vincent O'Brien was an organist in Dublin and John McCormack's first singing teacher.*

Boys' School who was entered for the Boys' Vocal Solo competition in April 1929. The test piece was the Irish song 'Cailin na Gruaige Donne' ('Girl with the Dark Hair'). Joe came fourth out of 53, with the first prize awarded to Edward Henry O'Doherty, son of one the founders of the Feis. Fourth out of 53 is not a bad result, and, since it was unusual for adjudicators at the Feis to award a fourth place, it may indicate that the adjudicator, Mr. Turner Huggard, wanted to acknowledge a pleasing, if not winning, performance.

Coincidentally, Edward Henry O'Doherty was also the boy who, as Joe later recalled, replaced him as principal treble in the cathedral choir after his demotion. As an adult O'Doherty was to enjoy considerable popularity as a singer in and around Derry, and even sang on the radio, but nothing to compare with the career of the boy he had beaten in the Feis.

In his final year at St Eugene's School Joe was entered for the scholarship examination for St. Columb's College, Derry's premier Roman Catholic senior school. Contrary to the later widespread assumption that Joe was no scholar or that he did not apply himself at school, he obtained an Irish Society Entrance Scholarship in July 1929 which entitled him to a year's free tuition at St. Columb's. We don't know whether he took up this scholarship and then had to drop out after a year because his family couldn't pay the fees, or whether lack of money meant that he couldn't go to St. Columb's in the first place. The 1929-31 School Registers for St Columb's College are missing, making it impossible to check if Joe was ever a pupil there.

Working Life

Whatever the reason for his leaving school, Joe spent the next few years in part-time jobs, all that was available to an unqualified young man in a city known for high levels of unemployment. According to Joe himself, his first job was plucking chickens at a poultry yard belonging to John Hume's uncle in Abbey Street. Later in his career, when he was already well established as a professional singer, Joe more than once branched out into pig-farming and horse-rearing, and generally showed an abiding interest in working with animals which may go back to this time.

Joe was typical of other young Derry men at this time in not finding a regular job and having to revert to a modified version of the farming economy: keeping chickens, rearing livestock and selling it on, and turning his hand to any odd-jobs that came up. In Joe's case, however, what made his situation worse was the break-up of his parents' marriage and the loss of the home in which he had grown up.

The Break-Up

We can't be sure what led Joe's parents, after thirty-plus years of living together and raising a family, to go their separate ways. Joe never spoke about it, an indication perhaps that it had affected him deeply in ways not easily gauged. In the highly charged

A street in Londonderry
The house where "Jo" was born

The McLaughlin family home at 19 Creggan Street where Joe grew up.

and puritanical religious atmosphere of Derry in the 1930s – puritanical on both sides of the religious divide – marital breakdown was something to be talked about, if at all, in hushed tones. That stigma, and Joe's reaction to it may explain, at least partially, his own troubled marital history, the failure of his three brief marriages and of his one longer term relationship. It may also explain the concern Joe showed for the children of those broken relationships.

The story that has come down within the McLaughlin family is that the break-up was triggered by the breach of a gentleman's agreement between Joe's father and the owner of the butcher's shop where he worked. Patrick McLaughlin had been promised that his job would be protected – and even that he would be given a part-interest in the shop – when the owner died. But when he died, his son didn't honour the agreement and promptly sacked Joe's father, putting him out of work.

The story receives at least partial confirmation from a report in the *Derry Journal* in November 1927. Patrick McLaughlin's landlord brought an action in the Derry Recorder's Court to recover possession of 19 Creggan Street – the McLaughlin family home – on the grounds that the tenant, Joe's father, had taken out the ground-floor front window and turned the house into a butcher's shop. Patrick's lawyer argued successfully against this that the previous landlord had told his client that he could do what he wanted with the property; that the removal of the window didn't involve any structural alteration to the building; and finally that his client had only taken this action because he had been thrown out of his regular employment.

The changes to the family home failed to arrest the decline in Patrick McLaughlin's fortunes. At the beginning of 1932 he could no longer afford the rent for 19 Creggan Street and the McLaughlins had to move in with Patrick's sister, Mary Jane Brown, Joe's 'Aunt Cissie', and her husband Jimmy around the corner in Creggan Terrace. Perhaps this was the final straw for Annie McLaughlin. It was around this time that she left her husband and went to England, taking her two youngest children, Anna and Dickie, with her. There, she went into service to support herself and the children. Of those left behind Thomas (Tom) was already married and settled in Derry; Brendan went to live with his god-mother. Joe and his father remained with Aunt Cissie for the meantime, although Patrick McLaughlin moved to England shortly after. As for Joe, he had still to decide about his future.

CHAPTER TWO

In Uniform
1934-1941

Joining Up

Derry in the early 1930s offered few opportunities for employment to someone like Joe who had left school without educational qualifications. The city had been in the grip of an economic downturn since the end of the First World War, with unemployment made worse by the Partition of Ireland. So much so that a Derry Employment Committee had been set up in 1922 to monitor unemployment in the city and in the neighbouring towns of Strabane and Limavady, and to press for measures to relieve it. In the early 1930s unemployment figures in Derry made grim reading: between 1930 and 1934 the number of persons unemployed in the city never sank below 2,600 and for most of that time was in the middle to high 3,000s. Of these roughly two-thirds were male. Nor was the situation any better in Northern Ireland as a whole where more than a quarter of the workforce were registered as unemployed.

Joe (pictured centre, without cap) in dress uniform with his fellow Irish Guardsmen in the mid-1930s
(By kind permission of the McLaughlin family)

With so little prospect of finding anything other than part-time jobs in his home town, and an industrial depression in England and the United States, it is understandable that young Joe should have seen enlisting in the British Army as a possible way out. Perhaps he had seen a series of adverts in the *Derry Journal* in 1930 and 1931 that were headlined "ARMY RECRUITS WANTED". They offered "men of good character, from 18 to 25 years of age, good pay, free food, clothing and lodging." There was the prospect of furlough on full pay; increased pay and rapid promotion for good men; participation in sports and games for all. Anyone interested was to apply to the local recruiting officer at the 'Barracks in Londonderry'.

There was a problem: in 1934 Joe was still only 17. But he was big for his age – well on the way to the six feet two inches he was later to reach – and managed to persuade the recruiting officer for the Irish Guards that he was a year older. His choice of the Irish Guards was a natural one for someone from Derry. The Guards, affectionately known as 'The Micks', drew the majority of their recruits from Northern Ireland and the Irish diaspora in the larger English cities; and notwithstanding the creation of the Irish Free State, even from south of the border.

Early days in the Irish Guards

On joining up in early October 1934 Joe had to report to the Guards' Training Depot at Caterham in Surrey for twelve weeks' basic training. It was familiarly known as 'Little Sparta' because of the fierce discipline enforced there. All recruits on arrival were given a medical inspection and assigned to a squad of a dozen men or more under a corporal drill instructor. The training consisted of 'square bashing' – learning to march together, wheel, halt and come to attention in response to barked orders – rifle drill, P.E. exercises, 'fatigues' or menial jobs of various kinds, mugging up on regimental traditions, and learning how to keep one's kit and uniform spick and span for regular inspections. At the end of the twelve weeks there was a 'Passing Out' Parade, when recruits such as Joe showed off the results of their training and were formally recognized as guardsmen, the Brigade of Guards' equivalent of privates. From Caterham they went on to Pirbright Camp for more specific battalion training, involving forced marches, long distance running with full kit, and special weapons training.

There are two photographs of Joe dating from his early days in the Irish Guards. The first, a studio portrait, shows him aged 17, seated, and wearing a heavy greatcoat buttoned up to the neck, a swagger stick and gloves in his left hand. His Guards' forage cap is perched on his right knee. The face is boyish and his dark curly hair, closely trimmed at the sides, stands up high on his head. The second, presumably later, shows him standing upright, chest out, in his ceremonial Guards' uniform, a trim figure, wearing the forage cap and with his Corporal's stripes or chevrons on his right sleeve.

Joe's Corporal's stripes show that his age at enlistment hadn't held him back. He was later to claim that, aged 18, he became the youngest Sergeant in the Brigade of Guards. That statement needs to be treated with caution. In his army records he appears as

The first studio portrait of seventeen year-old Joe as an Irish Guardsman. (By kind permission of the McLaughlin family)

Corporal J. McLaughlin, 2718060, Lance-Serjeant – a rank peculiar to the Brigade of Guards, the equivalent of full Corporal in other regiments. A Lance-Serjeant wore three white chevrons on his arm, but was distinguished from a full Serjeant whose three chevrons were gold. Joe may well have earned his promotion to Lance-Serjeant, but it didn't make him an NCO.

In the two years that Joe was with the Irish Guards in England the regiment was based in London, as indeed all the Guards regiments had to be, to carry out their ceremonial duties. In 1934 the Irish Guards were at Chelsea Barracks; in the following

Joe pictured (extreme right) in Cairo with two fellow Irish Guardsmen (By kind permission of the McLaughlin family)

year at Wellington Barracks near Buckingham Palace; and from September 1935 until the regiment's departure for Egypt in November 1936 at Chelsea Barracks again. Joe never spoke about the ceremonial side of his army career, although it was a major part of his duties as a guardsman in those years. The sole exception to this was a newspaper interview he gave long afterwards (in 1992 to the *Sunday Independent*) in which he said he was on guard when Edward VIII, "about to be demoted to the Duke of Windsor, was seen off from Buckingham Palace." But the story cannot be true – perhaps he was confusing it with some other occasion – since the Irish Guards left for Egypt in the middle of November 1936 and Edward didn't leave the Palace for Fort Belvedere, where the abdication took place, until 3 December.

The Foreign Years 1: Cairo

Joe's first experience of service overseas was in 1936 when the 1st Battalion of the Irish Guards was posted to Egypt. They sailed from Southampton on 14 November and disembarked at Alexandria eleven days later. They were stationed at the Kasr-el-Nil Barracks on the banks of the Nile in the centre of Cairo. Together with the 1st Battalion of The Royal Northumberland Fusiliers and the 2nd Battalion of the Cameron Highlanders, they formed what was known as 'The Cairo Brigade', part of a force of 10,000 British army personnel that the Egyptian Government had agreed should remain in the country to defend the Suez Canal.

Apart from the usual routines of barracks life – drilling, fatigues and inspection – there were occasional trips into the desert west of Cairo on training exercises – not a problem in the moderate temperatures of an Egyptian winter, but no joke in the blistering heat of the summer months.

A fellow guardsman recalled that Cairo had little entertainment to offer the off-duty soldier at that time: no dance-halls to meet girls or pubs to drink in. There was an open-air swimming pool in the barracks and a cinema, and the Army Education Corps ran daytime classes for the troops. There were visits to the pyramids and sailing trips on the Nile, and Joe even rode a camel. Nearby was the Egyptian Museum in Tahrir Square and the Gezira Gardens. For Joe it must have been, at the very least, an exotic contrast to life in London, to say nothing of his childhood days in Derry.

The Foreign Years 2: Palestine

However Joe's easy life as a peacetime soldier in Cairo was not to last. An Arab nationalist uprising against the British Mandate in Palestine reached its peak in the summer of 1938, and the Irish Guards were ordered to Palestine to reinforce the British military presence there. The battalion travelled overland from Egypt, an arduous journey of over 500 miles, passing over the Suez Canal and crossing the Sinai Desert at the height of the summer, before arriving at the railway junction of Lydda, north-west of Jerusalem on 12 July. Their camp was on the outskirts of Nablus, a town about thirty miles north of Jerusalem, one apex of the so-called 'Triangle of Terror' – the others being Jenin and Tulkarm – that was the centre of Arab resistance to British rule.

The main job of the Guards was to keep open the road between Haifa and Jerusalem and to remove any roadblocks set up by Arab guerillas, whom the troops called 'Ouzlebarts' or 'Ouzles', the squaddies' version of the Arabic word *asabat* meaning 'fighting groups'. It was dangerous work, as they often came under fire from snipers in the hills above. Another danger was mines: two guardsmen died in August 1938 when the army lorry in which they were travelling struck a mine on the road between Nablus and Jenin. The other job of the battalion was to carry out vehicle and house searches for concealed weapons. They generally acted in conjunction with the Palestine Police Force, which may have given rise later to the false impression that Joe himself joined or was seconded to the Palestine Police Force at this time.

The local Arab population, while not openly hostile to the British soldiers, were suspected of covert support for the uprising, and it wasn't judged safe for off-duty soldiers to venture beyond the limits of the camp. That would have put pressure on the Irish Guards to devise their own in-camp amusements. Hence, perhaps, the report in a 1950 newspaper that can only have originated with Joe, that his first ever concert was in Palestine during this time. While it didn't say what kind of concert this was, it was most likely got up by the troops themselves, with different guardsmen taking it in turns to sing, play a musical instrument, crack jokes, or perform tricks for the entertainment of the battalion as a whole. What lends credibility to the story is that a contemporary, Henry Martin of the Royal Army Medical Corps, said many years later that it was his claim to fame that he had sung with 'the famous Josef Locke' while serving in Palestine.

The Irish Guards were recalled from Palestine at the end of November 1938 and reached England in the week before Christmas. The role of the troops in combatting the Arab insurgency was recognized by the award of three military crosses and four military medals to individuals for 'gallant and distinguished conduct', and by a general service medal with 'Palestine Clasp' to all who had seen action there. Joe was later to claim that he been wounded in the leg while serving in Palestine and had to spend three months in hospital recovering.

Whatever the circumstances, Joe had now completed almost five years military service with the Guards and shortly after the return of the regiment to England – at all events, by early 1939 – Joe was back in Northern Ireland, looking to return to civilian life.

Home to the RUC

Joe applied almost immediately to join the Royal Ulster Constabulary, Northern Ireland's police force. At that time service in the British army – particularly with the Irish Guards – was often recommended to young men as a route into the over-subscribed RUC. It gave the applicant a head start over men applying from 'Civvy Street'. And Joe at 22, a fit 6' 2" ex-Guardsman who had seen active service abroad, had other advantages stemming from his Guards' training and insistence on smartness of turnout at all times.[1] Joe's initial interview for the RUC was on 16 February 1939, and one of those applying at the same time was (the later Head) Constable Irwin, who was stationed in Fintona in the 1950s. He recalled seeing Joe on the day of his entry interview at the RUC depot in Queen Street, Enniskillen "dressed immaculately in a pin-stripe suit, with trilby hat and umbrella… [He] looked the part in every way before the interview."

This was followed by a fitness test on 24 February 1939 which Joe passed with ease. What must have impressed the selection panel most of all was Joe's imposing physique and obvious physical fitness. Not only was he accepted into the police force, but his first appointment was as a Physical Education instructor at the RUC Depot in Enniskillen, an unusual first appointment for one so young. Joe would have been considered a 'godsend' to the RUC at this time, given his experience of drill in the Irish Guards.[2]

Joe's acceptance into the RUC was now complete, and all that remained for him to do was to return briefly to England to resign from the Guards and to purchase his discharge. This he did within a week, and on Friday 3 March 1939 Joe reported for duty as 'Constable 5349' at the RUC Depot in Enniskillen. Joe's 'buying himself out' of the Regiment – rather than merely leaving – proved fortuitous, as it exempted it from being recalled to the Guards at the start of the Second World War.

Joe's new post was not so far from his family in Derry and he soon attracted a certain amount of attention on his trips home by driving around in his own Ford car, at a time when owning a car was largely confined to the well-to-do. This was the start of a love affair with cars that was last for most of Joe's life.

'No Ordinary Tenor'

Although, as we have seen, Joe had sung before an audience on at least one occasion during his time with the Irish Guards, it was in Enniskillen that the quality of his singing voice was first recognized. In autumn 1939 Paddy Creegan, a local insurance agent and a member of the local St. Michael's Roman Catholic Church choir, was visiting the Enniskillen Depot on business when he overheard Joe singing in the barracks. Impressed by the power and sweetness of his voice, he invited him to join

---

[1] Although Joe often claimed to be 6' 2" in height, his Police Record from that time states that he was in fact just 5' 11".

[2] The RUC Training Depot in Enniskillen had only opened in 1936 and was still building up its training personnel.

St. Michael's Choir. At first Joe stalled, claiming not to know the Latin words of the liturgy. However, having attended Sunday Mass in St. Michael's for a couple of weeks as a 'silent worshipper' Joe allowed himself to be persuaded. At first he simply sang the Gregorian 'Missa de Angelis' with the other members of the choir, but Creegan had more ambitious plans for him. He gave Joe the vocal part of Gounod's 'Ave Maria' and arranged for him to practise it with Mrs. Rooney, a local pianist.

This paved the way for Joe's first documented solo performance. It was on 12 November 1939 when he sang 'Ave Maria' during the 11.30 Sunday morning mass at St Michael's. He sang it again at mass the following Sunday. The *Fermanagh Herald* reported that the congregation was delighted with the singing of the newcomer to the choir, which left them with "a wonderful and abiding impression of the superb range and quality of his rich and resonant voice." The highest and most difficult notes, it went on, were reached with clarity, sweetness and ease. Everyone knew straightaway that this was 'no ordinary tenor'.

One of Joe's duties during his time in Enniskillen was to lead a Sunday church parade from the Depot to the various churches of the town. They proceeded up Queen Street and left into Darling Street, where the Methodists peeled off into the pillared Methodist church. Then, at the top of Hall's Lane, the Church of Ireland contingent turned left into St Macartan's and the Catholics turned right into St Michael's. Joe himself turned right, ascended the stone spiral staircase to the gallery, and sang with the choir in full uniform.

On 12 December 1939 Joe had his first documented public concert at the Foresters' Hall in Enniskillen. Again he sang Gounod's 'Ave Maria', but with two other songs: the Irish ballad 'I Hear you Calling Me' and 'You are my Heart's Delight' from Franz Lehár's musical *The Land of Smiles*, songs associated with the celebrated tenors John McCormack and Richard Tauber. It was said that Joe 'brought the house down'.

'Constable McLoughlin' [sic] was then among the performers listed in advertisements for a follow-up concert in Enniskillen Town Hall on 29 February 1940, but he seems not to have played any part on the night. He may have been suffering from the tonsillitis that around this time prevented him taking up the offer of an audition with Radio Éireann set up for him by the tireless Paddy Creegan.

On 1 May 1940 Joe was transferred to the RUC barracks in Lisburn. He had spent just over a year in Enniskillen, and was always to retain fond memories of the place. Townspeople for their part remembered Joe as a modest and affable young man with a pleasing personality who seemed absurdly unaware of his own God-given talents as a singer. And despite Paddy Creegan's efforts to gain wider recognition for Joe, he had nothing more than a local reputation in Enniskillen, and a handful of public performances behind him.

Lisburn and Belfast Years

Joe's move to Lisburn brought a pay rise: he was now on a salary of fifteen pounds a month. As part of his official police duties in the town he was appointed 'honorary' drill instructor to the Local Defence Volunteers, the Northern Ireland equivalent of the Home Guard, a job for which his career with the Irish Guards and his work at the Depot in Enniskillen ideally fitted him.

In Lisburn, too, he soon made a name for himself as a singer. On Friday 15 November 1940, for example, there was a concert in the E.M.B. (Elise Milne Balfour) Hall in Hilden, just outside Lisburn, in aid of the 'British Sailors' Society. 'Mr. Joe McLoughlin' [sic] opened the proceedings with 'I'll Walk Beside You', and performed other unspecified songs in the second half. The following Friday 22 November, he was singing again, this time at a British Legion Supper in Lisburn Golf Club. Joe, the ex-Guardsman, seldom had to be persuaded to turn out for charitable functions, whether for ex-servicemen or, later in life, for his former RUC colleagues.

However Joe's singing was not universally welcomed. There's a story that Joe was drinking one evening in Lavery's Bar, then called the Maze Inn, in Chapel Hill in the centre of Lisburn, when he decided to entertain the company with his singing. The landlord objected, on account of his being too loud, and subsequently barred him from the premises.

It was while in Lisburn that Joe began to go out with a local girl, Esther (Essie) Woods McKeown. Joe was 23, Essie a year younger. She lived in Wallace Avenue, and worked as a shop assistant in Woolworth's in Bow Street. According to Essie, Joe often snaffled a few sweets from the counter when he came to see her in the shop. They could only have known each other for a few months when they decided to get married. But, at this time, Joe had to obtain permission from his RUC superiors to get married, and have his prospective bride vetted, to ensure that she was suitable to become a policeman's wife. Permission was granted, but with the proviso that Joe would be regarded as a 'single man' until he had completed five years' service.

'Happy Ever After'

Joe and Essie were married at Hillhall Presbyterian Church in Lisburn on the afternoon of Wednesday 19 February 1941. The local paper reported the wedding under the headline, 'Lisburn Bride for RUC Member'. Essie was 'given away' by her uncle, John Morrison; the two bridesmaids were her younger sister, Nan, and her cousin. After the church service, the wedding guests were entertained at Essie's family home in Wallace Avenue.

No mention was made in the newspaper of the fact that Essie was a Presbyterian and Joe a Catholic, nor do we know how the problems this might give rise to in a society as religiously polarized as Northern Ireland were to be overcome. Essie was later quoted as saying that, when they were married, Joe had agreed to 'go her way' – which could be taken as meaning that he had agreed to become a Presbyterian himself; or, alternatively, that he had agreed to let her 'go her own way', that's to say, he wouldn't put pressure on her to become a Catholic. This was to become a bone of contention between them later. For the time being, however, as we will see, Joe seemed happy enough to involve

Joe and Essie's war-time wedding in Lisburn on 19 February 1941. Joe is wearing his full RUC uniform. (By kind permission of the McLaughlin family)

himself in the musical life of Essie's church. She was later to remember him driving her to church on a Sunday morning in a pony and trap.

Within a few days of their wedding, on 1 March 1941, Joe was transferred to 'beat duty' with the police in Belfast and was stationed at the Leopold Street Barracks. According to Joe's police records, this was to reinforce police strength in the city in the face of recent IRA raids on banks and post-offices. But the move to regular police duties may not have been welcomed by Joe, used as he was to a freer, more independent role as drill-instructor. This, coupled with his failure to gain promotion, may have led to Joe's disenchantment with his life in the RUC.

In addition, it was while in Lisburn and Belfast that Joe acquired a reputation as the

The advert which Jimmy O'Dea placed looking for a singer for his Company in March 1941. (Irish Independent, 27 March 1941)

'Singing Bobby', from his singing when he was off duty at 'Smoking Concerts' and working men's clubs on a cash-in-hand basis. The former were men-only gatherings organized by the Temperance Movement, in an attempt to draw working men away from drinking in pubs. (Tobacco was then thought of as less harmful than alcohol, and smoking carried a certain veneer of sophistication.) Joe was no teetotaller, but neither was he averse to earning a little money in addition to his police salary. This juggling of police work with singing in clubs could hardly have escaped the attention of his superiors in the RUC, nor, when noticed, have been regarded favourably by them. It may have led to a growing tension between them and their maverick subordinate.

Audition at the Empire

The story of how Joe was 'discovered' by the Dublin comic actor and impresario Jimmy O'Dea has often been told, and over the years has taken different forms. We can discount some of the wilder versions: that it took place in Dublin's Gaiety Theatre; or at a talent show in a Belfast cinema; or that Joe just wandered in off the street and asked O'Dea to hear him sing. The reality was more mundane.

On 17 March 1941 O'Dea's company opened in Belfast's Empire Theatre with their pantomime *Babes in the Wood*. The lead male singer in the panto was the well-known Dublin baritone Robert Irwin. He, however, had made it clear to O'Dea that he would not be available to go on the company's planned spring tour of the south and west of Ireland. So, O'Dea placed an advertisement in the *Irish Independent* on 26 and 27 March: "WANTED – Male Vocalist, long tour Ireland; opening Easter. State terms, etc. to Manager, O'D. Productions Ltd., Empire Theatre, Belfast."

Joe himself said that O'Dea was looking for a replacement for Irwin, and the advertisement makes clear that what O'Dea had in mind was a short-term replacement for the coming spring tour not a long-term job with the company. Joe must have seen the advertisement or otherwise learned that O'Dea was looking for a singer and duly presented himself at the theatre. He was wearing his policeman's uniform, perhaps because he was either coming off or going on duty. First, he sang "I'll Walk Beside You' which he had sung at the concert in Hilden the previous November. Then, when O'Dea asked him if he knew something else in a higher range, Joe gave his by now well-honed rendering of 'Ave Maria'.

18

The Stage in The Empire Theatre in Belfast where Joe had his first audition in late March 1941. (Author's own collection)

O'Dea was sufficiently impressed to offer Joe £7 a week on the spot to join his company as the resident singer on their spring tour. Since Joe was only earning £15 a month as a policeman, this was a substantial inducement, quite apart from the appeal for Joe of earning his living as a singer. He straightaway agreed to hand in his notice to the RUC and to follow O'Dea down south. What his new wife made of Joe's sudden decision – six weeks into their marriage – to give up a secure career as a policeman for the risky and unpredictable life of a professional singer, we can only imagine.

And so, on 3 April 1941 Joe applied to be released from the RUC. Within the week he had received his last regular pay packet as a 'man in uniform', and was about to set off on the next phase of his life. In the event it was Joe's leaving Belfast in the second week of April to join O'Dea's company in the south that saved him from the greatest disaster ever to befall the city: the Belfast Blitz of 15 April 1941, when two hundred German bombers attacked military and manufacturing installations around the city. They destroyed or damaged 50,000 homes, leaving around 900 people dead and 1,500 injured, the worst loss of life in a single night in any British city outside of London. If Joe had still been in the RUC he would inevitably have been caught up in the mayhem, perhaps even among those who lost their lives. As it was, he had to learn about it at second-hand from the radio and Southern Irish newspapers. His thoughts may have been with the bombed city and with his young wife, but there was no turning back.

CHAPTER THREE

Learning the Ropes
1941-1945

Travels with O'Dea

Joe's new 'boss', Jimmy O'Dea, was an old hand on the Irish variety circuit. In his many years of touring, O'Dea had built up an unrivalled knowledge of Irish provincial audiences, knowing which towns to avoid and when. Youghal and Fermoy were 'poor' and brought in insufficient takings; while Cork, Enniscorthy and New Ross were all 'very good.' Joe had much to learn from him in stagecraft, in 'working an audience', and generally in how to survive and prosper as a variety artist in the harsh economic climate of war-time Ireland.

O'Dea had hired Joe to be the singer in his company for a ten-week tour of towns in the south and west of Ireland. The tour opened in Carlow Town Hall on Easter Monday. As fellow performer Vernon Hayden later recalled: "Joe knew absolutely nothing about theatre then" and he had to show him how to put on his make-up. From there O'Dea's Company went to Kilkenny, and through Tipperary to Listowel, Tralee and Killarney in County Kerry; turning south to the West Cork towns of Bantry and Clonakilty; then eastwards to Bandon, Youghal and Dungarvan; before finally striking north-westwards to Ennis and County Galway.

Joe's first job in the company was to keep the audience entertained during scene changes, with songs, wise-cracks and stories. This was when Joe first learned how to get the audience on his side, a trick that was to serve him well throughout his career. He had to learn quickly and in testing surroundings, while other members of the cast were noisily changing scenery behind him or groping around for changes of costume. In a small fit-up theatrical company like O'Dea's, everyone, no matter what their particular role in the company, had to lend a hand with any odd jobs that needed doing.

If Joe had thought that life as a professional singer would be a breeze, he was soon disabused. Wherever they went, he had to help build sets, shift scenery around, and generally act as a 'gofer' or dogsbody. That O'Dea wanted 'muscle as well as melody' (Joe's own words later) was something Joe hadn't reckoned on. This caused a minor flare-up near the end of the tour when the company arrived in Loughrea in County Galway. The hall they were to perform in was owned by the local undertaker, and the players had to improvise a 'stage' precariously on top of a row of empty coffins. Joe protested to Harry

Joe's first Dublin appearance
in the So What? revue in the
Gaiety Theatre in August 1941.

Gaiety Theatre

NIGHTLY at 8   MATINEE SATURDAY at 2.30

SO WHAT?

A COMEDY MUSICAL BY HARRY O'DONOVAN

Scene 1....Hollywood welcomes the New Stars
The M.C...Vernon Hayden

Scene 2...................................Jimmy meets Joan

Scene 3.."The Follies"
(1) Ballet.   Mary Poswolsky and Partner and the O'D Girls
(2) Ten Lullaby Lane.   Fred Doyle and Joan Reddin
(3) A Victorian Vignette.   The Singer, **May Devitt**

Scene 4.."A Ghost Story"
The Young Couple.................Jimmy O'Dea and M. Hayden
The Ghost Lady.......................................Maye Tipple
The Plumber..Albert Sharpe

Scene 5.......Joseph McLaughlin, the New Tenor

Scene 6........"Mr. Who" featuring Jim Johnson
with Vernon Hayden and Maye Tipple

Scene 7.................."Good Morning, Mr. Steen"
The Producer......................................Albert Sharpe
The Conductor.......................................Fred Doyle
Sally...**May Devitt**

Scene 8......................."It's all in the Script"
Vernon Hayden...............Reveals the Secrets of Broadcasting

Scene 9...Joan Reddin

O'Donovan, O'Dea's right-hand man, that he had signed up as a singer and not as a furniture remover. Nevertheless he stuck it out, learned some of the tricks of his new trade, and was a notable 'hit' with audiences on the tour.

How much of a 'hit' we can gather from the following review, written about the Company's visit to the theatre in Clonmel: "We were very pleasantly surprised by the appearance of a newcomer to the Company, Mr. Joseph McLoughlin [sic], a young singer who hails from Derry, and whom Jimmy told us he discovered during auditions which he held recently in Belfast. Mr. McLoughlin is a definite 'find', and should have a successful professional career. He has a lovely tenor voice, ample power, with a good range, and of delightfully sympathetic quality. He thoroughly deserved the ovation accorded him for his singing of 'I'll Walk Beside You', 'Danny Boy', and 'Smilin' Through'."

It was not only on audiences that Joe made an impression. Many of those he worked with on the tour became friends, not least Jimmy O'Dea himself with whom he forged a professional and personal relationship that was to last, whether they were performing together or not, until the latter's death in 1965.

Where was Essie, Joe's wife, all this time? She was later to say that early on in the marriage she had accompanied Joe on tour, but whether it was on this tour or on O'Dea's 1942 spring tour in Northern Ireland is unclear. In any event, Essie soon tired of life on the road and, after the fourth town visited, gave up and went home to Lisburn.

So What?

In mid-summer 1941 the O'Dea Company was back in Dublin and rehearsals started for a new O'Donovan revue *So What?* in which Joe was to make his Dublin début.

The show opened in the Gaiety Theatre in early August and ran for eight weeks to good reviews and the large audiences – the norm in Dublin's theatres in the war years. As a neutral country Ireland escaped the black-outs imposed north of the border, and its capital's theatres, clubs and cinemas did good business. Moreover in the absence of English and other stars from overseas, Irish entertainers had the chance to claim the limelight. Joe was lucky to be arriving in Dublin when he did.

In the course of the spring tour Joe had graduated from being a continuity singer to one of the company's leading performers. In *So What?* he appeared in three scenes, and as soloist in two of them, including the coveted final spot rounding off the evening. He was advertised in bold lettering as 'the New Tenor'. For the first time, too, Joe was backed by a top-rate professional ensemble, the Gaiety Orchestra conducted by Ernest Broadhurst. Apart from O'Dea, other members of the cast were dancer Mary Poswolsky, Joan Reddin, Jim Jonson and Jack Maguire; and someone who was to play a major part in Joe's life and career, Irish-born soprano May Devitt.

May Devitt

May Devitt was a petite dark-haired singer, thirteen years older than Joe. She was well-known in Dublin from having sung there in the early 1930s, before moving to England. She had come back to Dublin shortly after the outbreak of war. From her earliest performances with the Dublin Operatic Society she had been hailed as the city's up and coming operatic soprano, affectionately referred to as 'The La' (short for 'La Devitt') by her many friends and admirers. But no singer in Dublin could live by opera alone, and May also appeared in variety shows and pantomimes in Dublin theatres for impresarios like Jimmy O'Dea. She was married and had four young children.

May, along with O'Dea, was the star of the show; Joe at this point the young support act. But their duets in *So What?* that August and September were the makings of a partnership between the two singers that was to link their fates together over the next five years. But not immediately. At the end of the run, May went off to perform with Dublin Grand Opera and O'Dea took his show to the Opera House in Cork, where Joe's singing attracted favourable mention the *Cork Examiner*'s reviewer commenting of the newcomer that, "He has a very pleasing voice of good quality and volume, with a sympathetic interpretation." After a week in Cork, the show transferred to the Savoy Theatre in Limerick where Joe was again singled out for attention: "He has created a sensation everywhere he has sung."

In early November 1941 Joe parted company with O'Dea for the time being and went back north to Essie in Lisburn. Later that month he appeared as a guest artist in the Belfast Empire's long-running revue *Come to the Show*. It was his first

Dublin soprano May Devitt, photographed during her years singing with Joe. (Author's own collection)

professional engagement north of the border. The *Belfast News-Letter* praised this 'new tenor' and 'native of Londonderry' for his 'excellent tonal qualities' and 'interpretation of a high order;' and predicted that he would please Belfast audiences as he had previously delighted audiences in Dublin.

It must nevertheless have come as a shock to Joe to be back in Northern Ireland, where the rationing and nightly black-out – to say nothing of the bombed and derelict houses left by the Belfast Blitz – were stark reminders that this was a country at war.

A Year at Home

Since signing up with O'Dea in April 1941, Joe had been kept busy with a succession of singing engagements that left him only a few weeks of rest in-between. His career as a professional singer seemed well and truly launched. However, for some reason this was not carried over into 1942. So far as one can discover, his only extended term of work was in April, when he rejoined O'Dea's troupe who were making a short post-Easter tour of Northern Ireland.

They were in the Palladium Cinema in Coleraine throughout Easter Week, where the local newspaper reported that, "Joe McLaughlin, a young Derry man, made a particularly big hit." On the Friday, after the show, Joe took his chance to earn a bit on the side when he sang at a 'Special Cabaret Dance' in the Palladium Ballroom in nearby Portrush. During that week the seaside town – and its ballrooms – were been a-buzz with holiday-makers and possibly also with the American troops who had recently arrived in Northern Ireland, so this would have been an opportunity too good to miss.

Press ad for Joe's appearance with Jimmy O'Dea's Company in The Palladium, Coleraine in April 1942. (Northern Constitution, 4 April 1942)

PALLADIUM — COLERAINE.

SIX NIGHTS, commencing APRIL 6th.

6-45 — TWICE NIGHTLY — 9. O'D PRODUCTIONS LTD. PRESENT

A PERSONAL VISIT OF

JIMMY O'DEA

SUPPORTED BY

MAUREEN POTTER   JACK MAGUIRE and His Fiddle
(Late Jack Hylton's Band)
JIM JONSON Howya! Howya!
MAYE TIPPLE   :   VERNON HAYDEN   :   JOE CAREY
JOSIE DAY   :   SILVO (Harp)   :   TOM DONOVAN
JOE M'LAUGHLIN (Tenor)
HARRY O'DONOVAN   :   THE GAIETY GIRLS.

THREE COMPLETE CHANGES OF PROGRAMME—Monday & Tuesday,
Wednesday & Thursday, Friday & Saturday.

ADMISSION (including Tax)—Reserved, 2s 6d; Unreserved, 1s 3d.
Booking Office Open Daily.

The next stop on the tour was Ballymena, where they had a one-week run in the Town Hall starting on 13 April. O'Dea needed no introduction to Ballymena audiences, being already well-known from his Biddy Mulligan and Mrs. Murphy sketches on radio, and the local *Ballymena Observer* anticipated 'a mirth-provoking entertainment.' Among the other artists accompanying O'Dea, 'Joe McLaughlin' was picked out as "a tenor of exceptional merit [who is] already winning the plaudits of audiences."

From Ballymena O'Dea took his show to Belfast where it played ten nights in St Mary's Hall. The advert for the company's final performance noted that it was "prior to returning to the BBC Home and Forces programme." For O'Dea this meant travelling over to Bangor in North Wales, where the BBC's Variety Department was based for the duration of the war. It seems that Joe did not go with him, possibly because Essie was expecting their first child.

When we next hear of Joe, it was two months later in his hometown of Derry on 2 July 1942, where he topped the bill in a one-off *Show of Shows* in the Guildhall in aid of the British and American Red Cross. According to the *Londonderry Sentinel*, it was Joe who saw to all the arrangements, for what was a highly successful show. However, yet again this was followed by months of apparent inactivity or, possibly, domestic duties. (Joe's first child Yvette was born in November 1942.) It was not until December that Joe took part in three one-night variety concerts: in Caproni's Ballroom in Bangor, County Down, a venue popular with the American naval and military personnel stationed nearby; in the Beverleigh Club in Belfast; and again in Caproni's on Boxing Day.

In between these appearances, on Sunday December 20, he took the tenor solo part in Handel's *Messiah* in Lisburn First Presbyterian Church. This was Joe's most taxing singing role to date, and since, as he often admitted, his music reading skills were limited at that time, learning so much new music cannot have been easy. Musical friends in Belfast were later to say how much they admired his dogged perseverance in learning new music. He would sit up most of the night with a friend hammering out a piece on a piano

*Joe's first and only known
oratorio performance, in
Messiah in December 1942.
(Lisburn Standard, 18
December 1942)*

until he had mastered it. On this occasion he may have been coached by the *Messiah*'s conductor Winifred E. Thompson, who had formerly been a church organist in Derry, and could well have known him through her involvement with that city's Feiseanna.

The performance as a whole was praised in The *Lisburn Standard*, which described Joe's own contribution as 'polished' and added that "the range of his magnificent voice and its strength were equal to all the demands made upon it."

Come to the Show at the Belfast Empire

But after these few isolated engagements in 1942, Joe was soon in regular demand as a soloist at variety concerts in and around Belfast. In 1943 he appeared for nine weeks as a guest artist in different editions of the Empire Theatre's resident revue *Come to the Show*. In addition he was often the celebrity singer at various amateur talent competitions that were a feature of the entertainment scene in wartime Belfast, such as the heats of the Holy Cross Singing Competition in Ardoyne and the Super-Optimists' Golden Voice Competition in St Mary's Hall.

It was in spring 1943 that Joe was first heard as a soloist on the radio. Excerpts from the Empire show on 19 March were broadcast by the BBC on its 'For the Forces' Programme. This war-time radio station was principally for British servicemen and women at home and overseas, but civilians could tune in to it as well. There was a second 'Forces' broadcast from the Belfast Empire on 8 July, again with Joe singing. This was a special gala performance to mark *Come to the Show*'s Centenary Edition, in the presence of the Duke and Duchess of Abercorn, Sir Basil Brooke, and the Lord Mayor. On 13 August Joe was 'on the air' once more, this time as a solo artist in another 'Forces' programme *Irish Rhythms* with the soprano Mollie Millar and the Irish Rhythms Orchestra conducted by David Curry, over whom Joe – at six foot-two – must have towered. (Because of his small stature, Curry was sometimes jokingly referred to as 'the only leprechaun ever employed by the BBC'.)

By this time Joe and Essie's daughter Yvette was nine months old, and having to support a wife and child may explain the hectic schedule of performing Joe kept up at this time and his casting around for ways to increase his earnings. That was probably what lay behind a story that actor Noel Purcell told of the time that summer when he and Joe were performing together in Belfast's Royal Hippodrome Theatre. It was neither a great venue nor great pay, and Joe asked Purcell whether Louis Elliman, manager of the Theatre Royal in Dublin, could be persuaded to offer him £20 a week to perform there. Elliman didn't think Joe was worth that much and offered him £15 a week instead, which Joe turned down. It was something Joe and Noel would later laugh about in the 1950s when Elliman was paying 'Josef Locke' £1,200 a week to perform at the Royal.

Joe was also exploring ways of making money other than by singing. On Friday 11 June, he placed an advertisement in the *Lisburn Standard* offering 'Good Riding and Driving Horses and Ponies for Hire,' in which he promised that 'All the Animals [are] quiet', and claimed to specialize in teaching children to ride. The address in the advert was his parents-in-law's house in the town, 40 Wallace Avenue, where presumably he and Essie were living. This is the first indication we have of what was to become Joe's lifelong interest in horses, but the business was soon put on hold by changes in his private life.

According to Essie, one day in late summer 1943 Joe packed two suitcases and, without saying anything of his intentions, went out of the door, leaving her and baby Yvette behind. He had often been away from home before, when he was touring or performing down south, and it was not until some considerable time had passed without any word from him that she realized that he had gone for good.

In fact, he had not gone very far. Throughout the autumn he was singing at concerts in Belfast and doing week-long stints at the Empire in *Come to the Show*. Essie, left alone with a small baby, must have been distraught. But Belfast is a small place and it wasn't long before a rumour reached her that Joe was "keeping company with another woman in Belfast".

Joe's pattern of performing in 1943 was continued in the early months of 1944: the occasional variety concert in Belfast; being guest artist in *Come to the Show* at the Empire; and celebrity appearances at local amateur talent competitions. But in mid-February he achieved his goal, confided to Noel Purcell the previous summer, of a fortnight's booking at Dublin's Theatre Royal. Perhaps Elliman had had a re-think, or Joe had moderated his wage demands. He was to appear with May Devitt in a new revue *Royal Salute to 1944*. It may indeed have been May's influence with Elliman – for she was well-known to him and a great favourite with audiences at the Royal – that persuaded him to give Joe his chance.

Following his engagement at the Royal, Joe's career was to take a dramatic upward turn and this time almost certainly at May's suggestion. He was to appear alongside her in a forthcoming production by the Dublin Grand Opera Society (DGOS). There, May was very much in her element, having sung in opera since the mid-1930s, but for Joe this was something entirely new.

Operatic Debut

Joe made his operatic debut in Dublin's Gaiety Theatre on Wednesday 19 April 1944, in the tenor lead of Lieutenant Pinkerton in the Dublin Grand Opera Society's *Madame Butterfly*. May Devitt played the unfortunate Butterfly. It was generally agreed that they carried off the love scenes in particular with *éclat*.

There was something here the public was unaware of. Joe had little formal training as a singer and couldn't read music well enough to tackle an operatic score on his own. It was May Devitt with her classical training and knowledge of opera who took it upon herself to act as his *répétiteur*, going through each note, each aria and each duet with him until he had learnt the part by heart. By all accounts, Joe was a quick learner: it took him just two weeks to learn the role.

In many respects Joe suited the part of Pinkerton, the handsome but faithless young naval officer, to a tee. He was a commanding figure, over six feet in height, with thick dark wavy hair and glistening white teeth. He was at this time clean-shaven – the trademark Josef Locke moustache being something he grew only later. And he was once described as having 'strange blue eyes with indigo irises.' These manly good looks did not go un-noticed by the ladies in the audience, who trooped round in droves to his dressing-room after each performance to pay him compliments.

The professional critic in the *Irish Times* said of Joe's portrayal of Pinkerton: "He has a fine stage presence, and though new to the work, moves with natural grace." And of his voice: "He possesses a grand voice of warm vital quality, with great range, plenty of colour and reserve." Not bad for a twenty-seven year old ex-policeman who had never sung in opera before.

Although Joe was no stranger to the Gaiety and knew the stage manager, Tom Daly, and the other stage-hands from his time there with O'Dea's Company in 1941, he was caught out from time to time by the stricter social code of the DGOS. Once, at the first interval of *Madame Butterfly*, he was making his way to join the patrons at the bar, as he was 'dying for a cup of tea', when he was stopped in his tracks by the soprano Renée Flynn who sharply reminded him that audience and principals did not mix during a performance.

Joe's success with the Dublin Grand Opera Society brought him to the notice of the higher reaches of Dublin society. Although founded as recently as February 1941, the DGOS was by 1944 the premier music society in Ireland, drawing audiences from Dublin's wealthy and artistic elites. Among its patrons were Dr. John F. Larchet, Professor of Music at University College; Lady Talbot de Malahide; the art dealer Victor Waddington; Dr. Leonard Abrahamson, the eminent cardiologist; Eamonn O'Neill, T.D., Deputy Speaker of the Dáil; and Monsieur and Madame Louis Jammet of Jammet's Restaurant on Nassau Street. Its productions in the Gaiety Theatre were conducted by Commandant, later Colonel, James M. Doyle, of the Irish Army and Radio Éireann's Symphony Orchestra 'moonlighted' as its orchestra. It was a different world from the variety theatres with their popular programmes, scratch teams of musicians and working class audiences that Joe was used to.

Gaiety Theatre

Wednesday, April 19th and Tuesday, April 25th, at 7.45 p.m.

MADAME BUTTERFLY

GIACOMO PUCCINI
(By arrangement with G. Ricordi & Co.)

Dramatis Personae:

Cho-Cho-San (Madame Butterfly)...............MAY DEVITT

Suzuki (Cho-Cho-San's Servant)...........PATRICIA BLACK

Kate Pinkerton....................................ANNE FRAYNE

B. F. Pinkerton (Lieutenant in the United States Navy)
JOSEPH McLAUGHLIN

Sharpless (United States Consul at Nagasaki)
MICHAEL O'HIGGINS

Goro (a Marriage Broker)....................JOSEPH FLOOD

Prince Yamadori.....................................BEN ENNIS

The Bonze (Cho-Cho-San's Uncle)......RICHARD MASON

The Imperial Commissioner.........LUKE J. KENNEDY

Cho-Cho-San's Relations and Friends, Servants

Conductor..............................COMDT. J. M. DOYLE

Opera produced by SYDNEY RUSSELL

First produced: Scala, Milan, 1904
First produced in English: Moody Manners Opera Company,
Lyric Theatre, London, August 16th, 1907
Libretto by Luigi Illica and G. Giocosa

The programme for Joe's operatic debut in Madame Butterfly in Dublin's Gaiety Theatre on Wednesday 19 April 1944.

Yet Joe hadn't forgotten his beginnings. The day after his debut in opera he hurried back up north for a concert in Ballymena Town Hall. On the way, he stopped off in Belfast to take part in a BBC broadcast from the Empire Theatre to mark the 1000th performance of the revue *Come to the Show*. This was to become typical of him. All through spring and early summer 1944 he was juggling opera performances in Dublin and Cork with appearances at variety concerts up north.

Showboat at the Gaiety

Joe and May were soon singing together again, in the Irish premiere of the musical *Showboat*. It opened at the Gaiety Theatre on 3 July 1944, and was a lavish production with no expense spared. Joe was not originally supposed to be in the show, but the intended male lead, Heddle Nash, had to cry off at the last minute, and Joe was his replacement. It proved an inspired choice. In the opinion of the *Irish News*, "the selection of Joseph McLaughlin as Gaylord Ravenal [was] an excellent piece of type-casting." And indeed, had the public but known it, there was much in the character of Ravenal, the charming Tennessee swell, inveterate gambler, and wayward husband, that was to echo disturbingly in Joe's own life.

The Gaiety Theatre programme for Joe's appearance in July 1944 as Gaylord Ravenal in Showboat, his only known appearance in a stage musical.

These were of course the years of the 'Emergency' in Ireland when petrol was in short supply. As part of the publicity for the show Joe, dressed as Ravenal, drove May, his Magnolia, up Grafton Street in a horse and buggy. Years later Des Conway, the stage-doorman at the Gaiety, remembered them arriving at the theatre in a more homely style, with Joe on a bicycle and May alongside him in the carrier or sitting sideways on the bicycle-bar her long, dark hair blowing in the breeze.

Royal Bouquet at the Theatre Royal

The *Showboat* run ended on 29 July 1944, after record-breaking audiences and enthusiastic reviews, and Joe and May were immediately snapped up to appear again at the Theatre Royal. The revue *Royal Bouquet*, which ran from 31 July until mid-October 1944, was another production by 'T.R. Royle', an alias of Elliman's, with script-writer Dick Forbes. Joe and May, fresh from performing in opera and music theatre, were to provide singing at the higher end of the repertoire, alongside the usual medley of variety actors, comedians, and dancers. In the first few weeks they sang duets from *La Bohème*; later in the run it was selections from *Showboat*; later still, excerpts from Flotow's opera *Martha*; and in the closing weeks a musical selection, 'Wings of Song'.

Sometime that summer Joe seems to have felt remorse at having walked out on his wife the year before. He wrote to Essie asking her to join him in Dublin. She duly appeared there with Yvette, but the intended reconciliation – if that was what it was – didn't take place. According to Essie, they quarrelled about religion and she – good Presbyterian that she was – wouldn't give ground, and returned to Belfast that same day. Why Joe made an issue of this – so out of character, as it appears, with his generally relaxed attitude to religion – is something of a mystery.

'Singing Bobby' meets 'Singing Butcher'

Following the closure of *Royal Bouquet* Joe and May Devitt did two weeks with Jimmy O'Dea's Company in *Variety Fair* at the Belfast Hippodrome. They returned to Dublin at the end of October 1944 to begin rehearsing for the DGOS's autumn season. Joe had lead roles in two of the operas being staged: Ponchielli's *La Gioconda* and Puccini's *La Bohème* – more work behind the scenes, presumably, for May. By this time, though, May had put Joe in touch with her own voice teacher Vincent O'Brien, a man with considerable experience of training operatic singers (John McCormack was one of his pupils), and he may helped coach Joe in his new roles.

In *La Gioconda* Joe was cast as Enzo Grimaldi, a Genoese nobleman disguised as a seaman, and May played the eponymous ballad singer. Joe's rendering of the big aria 'Heaven and Ocean' was praised as 'highly artistic'. Altogether, the reviewer thought, "He has improved enormously, and although his acting is still somewhat stilted, one forgets it when listening to his resonant singing voice."

In *La Bohème* Joe and May played the parts of the young lovers Rodolpho and

Joe walking in a Dublin street in the mid-1940s. (By kind permission of the McLaughlin Family)

Mimi. The *Irish Times* reviewer was less fulsome on this occasion, noting that it was Joe's debut in this role, but that "he came through the ordeal creditably." His singing had 'a fine ringing tone', especially in the famous first act aria, and made up for the odd moments of uncertainty when he was singing along with others.

It was during this autumn opera season that Joe became friendly with another northerner, Belfast tenor James Johnston, who was lead tenor in other DGOS operas that autumn. Johnston was popularly known as 'the Singing Butcher' because he had started out working in his father's butcher's shop in Belfast's Sandy Row. (He was later to have a distinguished career as a tenor soloist with Sadler's Wells Opera in London.) Although their personalities and backgrounds were different – Joe the outgoing Derry Catholic and Johnston the shy, retiring Belfast Protestant – they were alike as singers in possessing great natural talent and little in the way of formal musical training. They had in common, too, that their fathers were both butchers.

A Night at The Opera

It was on 21 November 1944 in Dublin's Gaiety Theatre that Joe had his only recorded meeting with that other great Irish tenor, John McCormack, then at the very end of his illustrious career. McCormack was in failing health – he was to die within months of emphysema – but he was still one of the most respected figures in the musical world. It was often said afterwards that on this occasion he counselled Joe to concentrate on the lighter operatic repertoire and ballads for which his voice was particularly well-suited, much as he himself had done in his mid- to later years.

In truth, it wasn't quite like that. McCormack and his wife Lily had watched *La Gioconda* from their usual box overlooking the stage. After the performance they were invited onstage to meet the cast. As McCormack moved along the line of principals, he congratulated them on their performances that evening, with a few encouraging words for each. He stopped and spoke at length to May Devitt, a fellow pupil of Vincent O'Brien's, and known to be one of his favourites.

But when he came to Joe, his words were unexpectedly blunt. According to those within earshot, McCormack said to him, "As for you, McLaughlin, Grand Opera is not your forte." Joe himself later recalled him saying, "Maybe you were born on the wrong side of the Liffey – I don't know. But you can't sing opera." Whatever the exact words, there is no doubt that Joe took McCormack to mean he wasn't cut out to be a singer of the first rank, and that he should set his sights lower. Forty years after the event it still rankled. As well it might, since, if Joe's memory of McCormack's words is correct, they were a social, as well as a musical put-down.

Later, of course, Columbia records were to give the story a positive spin. In marketing Joe's early recordings of popular songs, they said that McCormack had taken a keen interest in the younger tenor's career and had pointed to popular songs and ballads as the way for him to go if he was to make the most of his talents.

Gaiety Theatre

LA GIOCONDA
(AMILCARE PONCHIELLI)
By arrangement with G. Ricordi & Co.

Dramatis Personae:

La Gioconda, a ballad singer......................MAY DEVITT
La Cieca, her blind mother.......................NORA FINN
Alvise, one of the heads of the State Inquisition
      RICHARD MASON
Laura, his wife...................................PATRICIA BLACK
Enzo Grimaldo, a Genoese Noble...JOSEPH McLAUGHLIN
Barnaba, a spy of the Inquisition...MICHAEL O'HIGGINS
Zuane, a boatman..........................JOHN W. DAVIDSON
Isepo, a public letter-writer ....THOMAS J. SYNNOTT
A Pilot.......................................LUKE W. KENNEDY

Monks, senators, sailors, shipwrights, ladies, gentlemen, populace, maskers, etc.

The Girls:—
Angela O'Connor, Gertie Coughlan, Gloria Dunfoy, Nanette O'Rourke, Cathleen O'Loughlan, Noreen O'Neill, Cora Doran, Tessie Timmons, Carmel Cultenan, Patty Gilligan, Marie Clarke, Rita Rackley, Mai Moloney.

The Boys:—
Nicholas and Joseph Connelly, Seamus Peelo, Louis Sheeran, Patrick McCabe, Brendan Moss, Maurice, Noel and Ronald Holmes, Edward Wilson, Thomas Coughlan, Patrick Gray, J. Barrett.

Conductor.................................COMDT. J. M. DOYLE

Original production by SYDNEY RUSSELL

First produced La Scala, Milan, April 8th, 1876
Libretto by Arrigo Boito, after Victor Hugo's play, "Angelo, Tyrant of Padua"
Time: 17th century   Place: Venice

A Night at the Opera: the programme for Ponchielli's 'La Gioconda' in November 1944, after which Joe met famed Irish tenor John McCormack.

The First Panto

After the high drama of romantic opera Joe and May were able to come down to earth for a few weeks, performing in the pantomime *Puss in Boots* at the Cork Opera House. May, as is the way in pantomime, had the travesty role of Prince Charming; Joe that of the Ogre. Joe Lynch, then a boy actor, later to become one of Joe's closest friends, also had a small part in the production. The pantomime opened on 26 December 1944 and ran until 13 January 1945. But, as before in Joe's Enniskillen days, the parishioners of St. Peter and Paul's Church in Cork had had advance notice of the quality of Joe's singing when he sang *Adeste Fideles* with the church choir at the Christmas mass the day before.

The panto over, Joe took a week's break in the north alone, when he was a guest artist on *Come to the Show* at the Belfast Empire. He then came down south again to meet up with May Devitt and a small troupe of other performers for a nine-week tour of country towns in the middle of Ireland that Joe and May had organized.

They called themselves *The Super-Optimists*, a name Joe may have 'borrowed' from the talent contests he had attended in Belfast two years earlier. And 'Super-Optimists' they must have been, given that they were proposing to travel from place to place by horse-drawn caravan and at what was usually the coldest time of the year. Here, at least, they were in luck. While January 1945 was one of the coldest months on record, February 1945, when they set out on tour, was the warmest February in Ireland since 1869.

'The Super-Optimists'

In the pre-tour publicity Joe and May were advertised as 'Ireland's Two Greatest Singers'. They were supported by a pianist, a yodeller, a 'Coon and his Banjo', an infant singer, a 'Ranch Boy' and a 'Personality Girl' – 'The Cream', or so it was claimed, 'of Belfast and Dublin Variety Stages'.

The tour started off with four nights in the Whitworth Hall in Drogheda, then travelled to a succession of small towns in the rural Midlands: Kells, Castlepollard, Mullingar, Edgeworthstown, Longford, Granard, and on into County Cavan. They played in cinemas, town halls, church halls and the halls of local institutes – basically anywhere there was a stage and space for an audience.

They were four nights in Virginia, County Cavan, and since that town had fewer than three hundred inhabitants, one must wonder whether 'The Super Optimists' had full houses there. But their presence would have been unmissable, as the convoy of horse-drawn vehicles moved from town to town, advertising their shows as they went. The tour ended in the Newbridge Picture Palace in County Kildare on April 8.

With the exception of Drogheda, where the concerts were reported in the local newspaper, it is difficult to know what Joe and May sang or how they were received. But there, at least, the tour seems to have gone down well. "Miss Devitt's singing," it was

Press ad for 'The Super-Optimists' Tour of rural towns and villages in Ireland during February 1945. (Westmeath Examiner, 10 February 1945).

COUNTY CINEMA
MULLINGAR

Thurs., Feb. 15,
Fri., Feb. 16,
Sat., Feb. 17, and
Sun., Feb. 18

JOSEPH McLAUGHLIN

MAY DEVITT

PERSONAL APPEARANCE OF IRELAND'S TWO GREATEST SINGERS

MAY DEVITT (Soprano) and JOSEPH McLAUGHLIN (Tenor)

IN THE MOST OUTSTANDING SHOW OF ALL TIME! PRESENTING:

THE SUPER OPTIMISTS

BERT MACK	JEAN HART	REG DALE
(Prince of Yodellers)	(Taps and Tempo)	(The Versatile Pianist)
MIKE FOX	JIM HAWTHORNE	BILLY LEE
(The Coon and His Banjo)	(The Ranch Boy)	(The Singing Infant)

said, "was a real treat and she was recalled several times." As for Joe: "Mr. McLaughlin's lovely tenor voice captivated the audience, and his repertoire, which included such favourites as 'Jerusalem', 'Goodbye' and 'Because', was a most popular one." There is no mention of arias or duets from the opera which Joe and May had been performing in Dublin. Perhaps the two singers reckoned that these would not have the same appeal for rural audiences?

Whether the tour was a financial success, we cannot say. What it did show, for sure, was that Joe and May were beginning to take charge of their own careers and were not going to wait around indefinitely to be offered opportunities to sing by others.

Ill-starred Lovers

In the meantime they were lined up to appear at the Gaiety in the DGOS's spring season. For Joe there was a new part to learn: he was to star with May in Gounod's opera of star-crossed love, *Romeo and Juliet*. There were to be repeats, too, of the three operas he and May had sung together the previous year.

Romeo and Juliet opened in Dublin on 7 May 1945, for three performances before moving for a final, single performance to the Cork Opera House. The *Irish Times* reviewer commented of Joe and May's performance as the young lovers that "their romantic rapport was convincing," and considered their duets in the second and last acts "among the best things they have done."

'Convincing' might have been under-stating it. By now it was known to some, and guessed at by many more, that the two were a 'couple' both on and offstage. And this relationship, no doubt, gave an extra frisson to their onstage appearances. An opera buff of the time summed it up, when he joked: "Sure we used to go to the Gaiety to see Joe's clinches with May." And Bill O'Kelly, the doyen of the DGOS, is said to have told Joe to 'cool it' onstage when his love scenes with May threatened to become too realistic. He took Joe aside after one particularly animated bedroom scene and warned him: "Cut out that business on the settee, Joe....It's a bit too bloody much."

Joe said that Romeo in *Romeo and Juliet* was the toughest part he had ever done. While he was later to claim that he had thoroughly enjoyed the experience of singing in opera, it is possible he was coming to realize that – as McCormack had said – grand opera was not where his strengths lay. Some critics were already murmuring that the top of Joe's voice was 'too light and too thin to cope with the heavier operatic roles'; although it was also generally agreed that what Joe lacked in technique and ability to sustain the high notes was made up for by his stage presence and charisma.

London Beckons

By early summer 1945 the war in Europe was over and the war in the East coming to an end. As for Joe, despite his successes in opera, he was beginning to feel the pinch. "There was no money in it," he would say, "We were getting just ten pounds for a whole opera." He made the same complaint to fellow tenor James Johnston: "For God's sake, Jimmy, the money's no good. I'd starve to death on it." He was already, it seems, looking to England and the money to be made in variety there. Nor did this come as a surprise to those in the DGOS who knew him well. O'Kelly, its Chairman at the time, was understanding: "I knew that we couldn't keep [Joe] in Ireland and that opera would never be his goal..... He was made for the variety stage. But he hadn't let me down and for that I was very grateful."

Joe was offered the lead role of Cavaradossi in Puccini's *Tosca* for the coming autumn, but his mind was already made up and he turned it down, and instead set off for London. May Devitt, his partner, confidante and teacher, gave up her life in Dublin to go with him.

Joe and May Devitt in the title roles of 'Romeo' and 'Juliet' in Gounod's opera in Dublin's Gaiety Theatre in May 1945

CHAPTER FOUR

'Blaze Away'
1945 -1950

Early days in England

The easing of war-time travel restrictions in summer 1945 meant that concert artists and other stage performers were once again free to move around Britain and further afield, opening up new worlds of opportunity. Joe and May joined a number of Irish singers, actors and artists who crossed over from Dublin to England at this time. They faced stern competition. The ENSA performers who had been entertaining the troops at home and abroad were already looking for peace-time jobs in London and the provinces; and demobilization had freed up others in the armed forces who had set their sights on a stage career. This, then, was the tough background against which Joe started his singing career in England and where, during the next five years, he made his meteoric climb to the top.

In the event, the two Irish singers didn't have unduly long to wait before finding work. Within a few weeks they were signed up by Jack Hylton, the band-leader-turned-impresario, who offered them a spot in his *Salute to Variety* show in the Victoria Palace in London. There, as Joe later told the story, when he turned up for rehearsal and saw the billboards advertising 'Josef Locke' and not 'Joseph McLaughlin', momentarily his heart sank, thinking that someone else had been booked in his place. However Hylton explained to him that the name 'Joseph McLaughlin' had to be shortened to fit the space on the advertising hoarding, and that, in any case, no one in London knew how to pronounce 'McLaughlin'. So 'Josef Locke' it was, and 'Josef Locke' Joe was to remain for the rest of his professional career.

Initially Joe and May were engaged for just one week, starting on 8 July 1945, but audiences and reviews were encouraging, leading Hylton to retain the duo for another fortnight. This first booking led to more engagements, and in the next few months they were rarely out of work. Their next booking was at the Dudley Hippodrome in the Midlands on 14 August. This was one of the newest and largest theatres in the Northern circuit, and engagements to perform there were greatly prized. Then in September they got a week's work at the Plymouth Palace, where they were advertised as 'celebrated opera stars'. They had a two-week engagement in early October at the Preston Hippodrome. Their programme there included arias and duets from *Traviata* and *Trovatore*, operas

PALACE VARIETIES

6-0 —— TWICE NIGHTLY —— 8-10.

THE BIG BROADCAST — THURSDAY (SECOND HOUSE).

FIRST APPEARANCE HERE.

FORSYTHE

JOSEF

LOCKE

AND

SEAMON

MAY

AND

FARRELL

DEVITT

FAMOUS IRISH OPERA STARS.

THE FAMOUS B.B.C. COMEDY TRIO.

Famous International Dancer.

EDNA SQUIRE

6 ANNETTE'S
PALACE STARLETS

BROWN

In "DANCE OF THE DOVES."

VESTA & ASHTON

Queen of Versatility.   King of Clowns.

Damzel & Partner

Tricks and Catches

BERT	TOMMY	CLEEF
NICOL	REILLY	AND
AND	and FRANKIE	MORONEY
MERRILL	STILL	Dominion
"Fooling For You."	"A Musical Furore."	Acromedians.

ALL SEATS BOOKABLE (EXCEPT GALLERY).   PHONE ONE.

Joe's first appearance in Blackpool on Monday 22 October 1945. (West Lancashire Evening Gazette, 24 October 1945)

38

which Joe had not performed in Dublin, and in which, one supposes, May Devitt had to coach him in the words and music.

The *Lancashire Evening Post* praised the two singers for the 'polish and charm' they brought to what was essentially a variety show: "Outside operas one rarely has the pleasure of hearing voices of such fine quality."

Blackpool Debut

Next was Blackpool, where in the last week of October 1945 Joe and May performed in a variety show at the Palace Theatre. Although at the tail-end of the summer season, it was Joe's first appearance in the town where he was to become a legend. Joe and May appeared second in the billing, a sure sign that they were beginning to be better known. On Thursday 25 October part of the show was broadcast on the BBC Light Programme in the weekly series *Northern Music Hall*. Although Joe had been heard singing on the Forces' wavelength and Northern Ireland radio on several occasions in the early 1940s, this was his first broadcast on the national network.

After another one-week stint in early November in the Coventry Hippodrome, Joe and May went into rehearsal for what was their longest engagement to date: ten weeks in the Howard and Wyndham pantomime *Goldilocks and the Three Bears* at the Royal Court Theatre in Liverpool. May had the part of Prince Valentine, Joe that of 'Orson, the Wild Man of the Woods'. The panto opened on Saturday 22 December 1945 and received rave reviews.

The *Liverpool Evening Express* hailed it "a triumph… a grand production which has everything." May was a 'lovely soprano… dashing and captivating' with an almost limitless supply of stunning costume changes. Joe was not so lucky in that department, having to spend most of the panto clad only in a leopard skin. Although

playing the part of the Wild Man, he was 'far from repulsive' and presented, the *Liverpool Daily Post's* reviewer thought, an 'imposing Tarzan-like figure'. This was just as well, since, in a surprise twist in the Liverpool theatre's version of the story, Orson and Prince Valentine turned out to be long-lost twin brothers, and ended each evening embracing one another. Joe's 'strong tenor voice' was singled out for praise, especially in his duets with May.

Joe as 'Orson, the Wild Man of the Woods' in Goldilocks and the Three Bears, the 1945 pantomime in Liverpool's Royal Court Theatre. (Liverpool Evening Express, 21 December 1945)

Press advertisement for Joe and May Devitt appearing at Hull's Tivoli Theatre (Daily Mail, April 27, 1946)

When the pantomime closed in March Joe and May were briefly back in Ireland for a BBC Radio broadcast from Belfast on Friday 22 March. Recorded at the Ritz Cinema, it was on the *From the Regions* show on Northern Ireland Radio. The accompanist was another Josef, the organist Josef Seal on the 'mighty Compton', the Ritz's cinema organ. Then, it was back to England where the couple were kept busy during April and May, with appearances in variety shows in theatres throughout England: in Oxford's New Theatre, the Wolverhampton Hippodrome, Hull's Tivoli Theatre and the Palace Theatre in Plymouth. Part of the Tivoli Theatre show was broadcast live by the BBC in *Northern Music Hall* on Thursday 2 May 1946.

Their next engagement was a big step up: appearing in the *Starry Way* revue in Blackpool's re-opened 'New Opera House', a magnificent extravaganza designed to celebrate the resort's first year of entertainment in peacetime. George Formby, then the biggest name in variety, topped the bill, with other stars, such as the exotic, transatlantic movie star, Movita. The local *Evening Gazette* was unstinting in its praise of the show, describing it as 'glittering with pre-war splendour... [right up to] ...its final fanfare in gold'. Joe and May in the "exquisite Viennese pastel [sic] and Venetian masque sang with a lyrical richness rarely heard in revue. They have the grand manner."

Joe's 'grand manner' – and his stoicism too – were put to the test during the run, when he had to go onstage wearing a sling and with his lower arm in plaster, the result of an accident while starting his car, when the cranking handle kicked back and broke two bones in his wrist. The local press was full of sympathy and admiration for his gutsy effort to convey 'gaiety, romance and glamour' while in pain. But it could also be that Joe, knowing the revue was being broadcast live on the BBC Light Programme that evening, wasn't going to pass up the chance of being broadcast in a show with George Formby as the lead.

For all their success as a duo in *Starry Way*, it was to be the last time that Joe and May were to partner each other on stage. Since coming to England they had largely confined themselves to singing the kind of operatic arias and duets they had performed together in Ireland, and perhaps Joe could see his repertoire and career developing in a different direction. Or perhaps their relationship had run its course and May recognized that fact. During the run of the revue in Blackpool that summer Joe had started to notice one of the young female dancers in the chorus, and May, like the Marschallin in *Rosenkavalier*, could have seen the writing on the wall.

Doreen McMartin

The young dancer in question was Doreen McMartin, a Lancashire girl. Although just twenty-one years old, Doreen was already a veteran of the Blackpool stage, having made her debut as a child performer in a Blackpool pantomime eight years earlier. She and her sister Olga had been dancing in pantomime and revues ever since.

Joe – one could be forgiven for forgetting – was still married. His wife Essie was living in Lisburn with their daughter Yvette. In September he wrote her a letter saying that they had now lived apart for three years and suggesting they divorce. It seemed to him that they were ill-suited to one another; that their marriage had been 'a tragedy and a failure; and that it would be better for them to go their separate ways. As for himself, he said, he had met no one he would want to settle with, his life as a 'wanderer' not being conducive to a settled life with anyone. If Essie would agree to the divorce, he would let the child remain with her – closing the letter, "Give my love to Evette [sic] and let me know if she needs anything. Yours as ever, Joe"

In November 1946 Joe was back in Northern Ireland again to perform in a number of charity concerts. He sang at a dance for his former RUC colleagues in the Plaza ballroom in Belfast on Tuesday 5 November. On the following Thursday as 'Joseph McLaughlin' he gave a concert for the Londonderry Savings Committee in Derry's Guildhall with local musicians, violinist Orlando Cafolla and pianist James Moore. Later that month Joe gave three more concerts on successive nights, again in the Guildhall, in aid of The Eye, Ear and Throat Hospital. In between, he revisited other old haunts to give an 'All-Star Concert' in the Town Hall, Enniskillen in support of 'The Graan', a Roman Catholic seminary and retreat house.

Joe photographed outside London's Blarney Club in the later 1940s with Doreen McMartin, (extreme right).
The Club belonged to Mayo-born Mick Gannon.

His September letter to Essie seems to have had its effect. On 19 December 1946 she petitioned for and was granted a divorce on grounds of desertion in Belfast High Court. Joe did not appear in court nor did he contest the action. He was, one supposes, relieved at the outcome and happy to be able to marry again. He could spend Christmas quietly with Doreen, free for the first time in three years from having to perform in pantomime.

They were married on 28 February 1947 at the Catholic Sacred Heart Church in Durham. The speed with which this happened, so soon after the granting of the divorce decree *nisi* in the Belfast court, was to have unforeseen consequences five years down the line. Their impatience at the time may have something to do with the fact that Doreen was already pregnant with their first child. After the wedding she devoted herself to being Joe's wife and mother of their children. She would never again dance professionally on stage.

The Break-Through Year

1947 was Joe's break-through year in England. He was signed up by Lew and Leslie Grade Ltd., then the UK's most successful light entertainment agency, which took over the professional management of his career. They secured him bookings with the country-wide Moss Empire theatres and encouraged him to develop the light tenor repertoire that was to become his trademark. Lew Grade in particular is often credited with advising Joe to forgo receiving a fixed wage from promoters and instead to take a percentage of the house takings. With Joe's steadily increasing drawing power this proved astute and far-sighted.

George Formby had been greatly taken by Joe's singing in *Starry Way* the previous summer, and with his backing Joe was able to obtain a recording contract with the Columbia Record Label. (Formby was already a Columbia recording artist.) Joe's first recordings, on 14 March 1947, a few days before his thirtieth birthday, were two Italian songs 'Santa Lucia'

Joe's first record with Columbia in 1947: a 78rpm featuring the songs 'Santa Lucia' and 'Come Back to Sorrento'

and 'Come Back to Sorrento'. He was accompanied by a full orchestra conducted by George Scott Wood.

Columbia had carefully chosen these songs to launch Joe as a recording artist. The record-buying public had long associated really fine tenor singing with the Italian operatic tenor tradition of Caruso and others, and notably in the 1940s with Beniamino Gigli. So having a relatively unknown but foreign-sounding Josef Locke sing Italian songs chimed in with people's expectations. They also played to Joe's strength, his seemingly effortless ability to reach high notes, and allowed him to indulge in the portamento effects and other embellishments characteristic of the Italianate singing style.

During the same studio session Joe recorded two more songs, one of which, the rousing 'Goodbye' from the musical *The White Horse Inn*, was to become his closing number in concerts and shows over the next fifty years. The 'B' side of this second record was the Richard Tauber song 'My Heart and I' from the musical *Old Chelsea*.

Sales of the first record, released in August 1947, were so good that Columbia brought him back to do more recordings on 25 September. These were 'I'll take you home again Kathleen' and 'Hear my Song, Violetta', and – with an eye on the Christmas market – 'The Holy City' and the Christmas carol 'Star of Bethlehem'. 'Hear My Song, Violetta' was a skilful re-working of a fragment of Violetta's aria from Verdi's opera *La Traviata* as a romantic ballad. More than any other song Joe recorded, it was to be the one with which his name became most closely identified.

1947 was also the year that radio 'discovered' Josef Locke. While he had previously been heard in live broadcasts from theatres where he and others were performing, the ease with which he could project his voice to a radio audience suddenly made him a popular choice as a named soloist in variety programmes on the BBC Light Programme. His first engagement of this kind was on Tuesday 18 February 1947 in the wavelength's *Happidrome* show. He was to appear another four times on the show before the year was out.

All this time Joe was continuing to appear twice-nightly in variety, but now topping the bill, in Moss theatres in the Midlands and north-east of England. In May 1947 he was back in Blackpool rehearsing for Tom Arnold's comic revue *Ev'ry Time You Laugh* in Blackpool's Opera House. It ran from 24 May until mid-September, and was a lavish production with elaborate scenery, costumes and dance routines. Arnold, a Londoner, knew the entertainment world, and appreciated that cinema, which had almost killed off variety in the later 1930s, could only be countered by pulling out all the stops in personnel and presentation. His 1947 show featured a number of international artists and a chorus and ballet of fifty performers. Glowing tribute was paid by one reviewer to "the persuasive voice and assured artistry of Ireland's Josef Locke [which] makes old things new and new things attractive."

At the end of this revue run, in later September 1947, Joe and Doreen's first daughter was born; the couple named her Moira.

From Vinyl to Celluloid

Earlier that year, when Joe was appearing in variety at the Garrick Theatre in Southport, he had been approached by representatives of John E. Blakeley, the founder and Managing Director of Mancunian Films, a local (Manchester) film company specializing in low-budget feature films with mainly northern actors. Always on the look-out for new talent, Blakeley wanted to secure Joe's services for a short comedy film *Holidays with Pay* about a Lancashire family's trip to Blackpool.

Filming started late in September 1947. Frank Randle and Tessie O'Shea were the lead characters. The plot, such as it is, consists of a series of comic episodes featuring Randle and O'Shea, linked incongruously to a melodramatic failed bid to murder the heir to a family fortune. Many scenes were shot on location in Blackpool itself, which gave the film added appeal for Northern audiences. Joe's contribution came in a cameo appearance, set in a saloon bar in the American west, where he plays an Irish cowboy Paddy Quinn and sings a romantic cowboy number 'Moonlight on the Prairie'. Nothing much in the way of acting was required of him and he didn't disappoint.

In the next eighteen months Joe appeared in two other Blakeley films, both low-budget comedies, with slapstick humour and Joe's singing as the key selling-points. Only a few scenes from the first film, *Somewhere in Politics*, have survived and Joe doesn't feature in them. It was apparently a satire on local government in which Joe played the part of a sitting town councillor who is challenged for election by one of his employees (Randle) egged on by his wife (O'Shea). The second film, *What a Carry On* survives only in a shortened version. Joe plays the part of Sergeant-Major Locke trying

An advertisement for Joe's second film, Somewhere in Politics *(Author's own collection)*

to drill some semblance of military discipline into two wayward army recruits (the comedians Jimmy Jewel and Ben Warriss). This was a role Joe was familiar with from his days in the Irish Guards and the RUC, so he is given more to do than in *Holidays with Pay,* but his is still an awkward performance. In a party at the Adjutant's home he gets to sing 'Le Rêve Passe' and at an army concert – a scene now lost – he sang 'Ave Maria' and 'Abide with Me'.

These, like Blakeley's other films, were very popular at the time with northern audiences and made him a lot of money. But their threadbare plots and reliance on northern comedy actors with their familiar routines and accents limited their appeal. As for Joe, he only seems at home in them when he is singing, and the songs themselves (chosen from his familiar repertoire) were tangential at best to the film's storyline. Whether he would have been more convincing in a later film *The Irish Emigrant* that Blakeley was planning, we will never know, since the project seems to have fizzled out before filming started.[1]

Paradise Parade and *Coconut Grove*

Early in October 1947 Joe embarked on an eight-month tour of the country in a new Jack Taylor revue *Paradise Parade*. Lancashire-born Taylor was another experienced producer of revues and pantomimes with a track-record of successful productions that assured him access to the better-rated venues. *Paradise Parade* opened in the Winter Gardens, Morecambe, and then went the rounds of the Moss Empire theatre chain: to Sunderland, Nottingham, Leeds and Birmingham. There was a hiatus from just before Christmas to the end of February 1948, when Joe and the other members of the cast took time off to appear in pantomime. In Joe's case, he was the Emperor in *Aladdin* at the Garrick Theatre in Southport. It was simply non-stop performing.

At the beginning of March the company re-formed, and took the show north of the border to the Edinburgh and Glasgow Empires. Then in April and May they toured other Moss theatres in the south of England (the Finsbury Park Empire, the Brighton Hippodrome); Wales and the Midlands (Cardiff's New Theatre, the Wolverhampton Hippodrome, the Swansea Empire); and finished this part of the run back in Lancashire at the Manchester Hippodrome.

As with previous Taylor shows, the keynotes were 'laughter and song'. The comedian Dave Morris set the tone with a series of comedy sketches, including one on the black market – a familiar topic in those days of post-war shortages and rationing. There was an athletic Apache dance and parades of dresses and furs by the 'Paradise Beauties'. Joe provided the singing, his choice of songs – as in the Blakeley films – quite unrelated to the topics of the revue. They were generally his latest record releases, but those, of course, were exactly what audiences wanted to hear from him.

---

[1] *"John E. Blakeley is to go into production in October next with Josef Locke in a story specially written around the ballad 'The Irish Immigrant'. Mr. Locke will be assisted by the Gaelic Choir of 100 voices, and specialities will be provided by 50 Killarney Colleens and the Donegal Pipers. Musical arrangements will be directed by Barney Finnegan." The Stage April 6, 1950.*

For the Blackpool 1948 summer season Taylor came together with Tom Arnold to put together another revue show, *Coconut Grove* at the Hippodrome Theatre. For this they draped hangings all round the interior of the auditorium aiming to recreate the atmosphere of the Cocoanut Grove nightclub in Hollywood which had fired his imagination on his recent trip to America. There was a strong American/Latin-American flavour to many of the acts. There were the Copacabana Girls in 'Braziliance' and a Latin American Orchestra to provide 'Cuban Rhythm'. Joe himself had three slots: 'Mexican Serenade', 'A Hollywood Fantasy' and 'The Girls of the Silver Screen'. Not least of the revue's attractions were artfully-arranged tableaux of semi-nude young women. (In the 1940s censorship by The Lord Chamberlain was strictly enforced in British theatres, and partial nudity, justified as always in the name of art, was allowed on stage only so long as the young women in question didn't move.)

The Blackpool season over, Joe took a break from singing and paid a visit home to Derry. But even on holiday he couldn't resist giving a concert in the Guildhall on 6 October for the Supporters' Club of the local football team, Derry City. He resumed touring with the *Paradise Parade* show at the Croydon Empire at the beginning of November; and stayed with the company when it moved on to the Palace Theatre in Plymouth and the Theatre Royal, Chatham; before again going into rehearsal for pantomime – once more in the role of the Emperor in *Aladdin*, but this time at the Middlesbrough Empire.[2]

Joe's reputation on the variety circuit by this time was such that he was routinely described in advertisements and revues as 'Britain's Greatest/Foremost/Leading Tenor'. When he appeared in Chatham – but here we must make allowances for the hyperbole of the advertising industry – Joe was 'England's [sic] greatest radio and recording star of the century'.

Getting a Slice of the Action

By the late summer of 1948 Joe's career was on a roll. He had made a number of successful recordings, his first film was showing in cinemas, he had topped the bill in variety in some of the biggest and best theatres around the country, and he had three full Blackpool seasons under his belt. He must, one would think, have been brimming with confidence. He would also have had a shrewd idea of the money to be made in the entertainment business at this time. Blackpool in the immediate post-war years was at the zenith of its popularity as a holiday resort, and Joe had seen the thousands of holiday-makers who flocked twice-nightly to the shows at various venues around the town.

---

[2] *Fifty years later one of the girls in the show recalled Joe with affection: "When I was in my 20s I used to work in shows and pantomimes with Josef Locke. What a decent man he was. Once, I was in panto Aladdin at Middlesbrough with two other girls from Blackpool. Josef was living in in Blackpool with his first [sic] wife and child at the time. He used to take us girls after the end of the performance on a Saturday night with him to Blackpool to be with our parents for the weekend and pick us up on Monday morning and take us back."*

As his past history showed, Joe had never lacked the spirit of enterprise. So on 4 August 1948, he set up and registered a private agency 'Josef Locke Ltd', to supply theatrical performers and variety artists to the entertainment industry. The new company had capital of five hundred pound and a registered address at his home, 536 Queen's Promenade, Blackpool**.** Joe and Doreen were listed as the sole joint permanent directors. An advertisement bringing the new agency to the attention of potential clients appeared in *The Stage* journal on 2 September.

The fruits of this new venture were not immediately apparent. But in March of the following year, the veteran comedians Syd and Max Harrison began touring a show *Tell 'Em All about It* , advertised as 'in association with Josef Locke' – Joe's first outing as a promoter. Not only did the show appear under his name, but there was a male vocal group, 'The Josef Locke Singers', an integral part of the show's appeal throughout its year-long run through the provinces. Joe himself never sang with the group, and was indeed often fully engaged elsewhere, but their name clearly indicates that they were under his management. We hear no more of them after the show closed in November 1949: so either the business of managing such a group was more trouble, or was less profitable, than Joe had anticipated.

London Highlights

In the early months of 1949 Joe was busier than at any time in his career so far. Joe had begun the year in the pantomime *Aladdin* in the role of Abanaza in Middlesbrough; and then appeared in the same production in the Liverpool Pavilion until the end of the first week in February. At one particular performance in Liverpool, Joe failed to turn up and his understudy went on instead. The next night, expecting the same, the understudy walked on to one side of the stage as Joe walked on to the other… and, to the bemusement of the audience, both burst into song simultaneously. But from 14 February onwards there was no let-up. He was singing twice-nightly, six nights a week, week after week, travelling to Edinburgh, Glasgow, Nottingham, Newcastle, and Brighton. The culmination of these weeks of unremitting effort was a three-week run at the London Palladium, starting on 21 March. This recognition of Joe's growing reputation must have been particularly gratifying to him, since he had not had a booking at one of the big central London theatres since his appearance as an unknown singer with May Devitt at the Victoria Theatre four years earlier. What is more, the Palladium's Managing Director Val Parnell was a dominant figure with a track-record of favouring big-name American stars over home-grown talent. But, if Joe was delighted to be on the bill, he was not overawed. Warned beforehand that Parnell didn't want him to include 'Galway Bay' among the songs he was to sing, Joe ignored the hints. And when Parnell insisted, on the afternoon of the opening night, that Joe drop the song and sing something else instead, Joe picked up his music and said, "Then I hope you can bloody well sing, Mr. Parnell, because if 'Galway Bay' isn't in, I'm out" and stomped off to his dressing room. Parnell eventually gave way and Joe got to sing 'Galway Bay' – to thunderous applause – but Parnell never forgave him.

Joe's debut performance at the London Palladium on 21 March 1949, less than four years after his arrival in London as a fledging tenor.

Programme

1. OVERTURE   -   -   *"Sunny Side Up"*

2. CHRISTIAN'S DOGS -   - *A Riot of Fun*

3. ALAN CLIVE   -   -   *The Host of Stars*

4. THE SEVEN ASHTONS *Australian Acrobats*

5. HARRISON, CARROLL & ROSS
Fast & Furious

6. JOSEF LOCKE - *Britain's Foremost Tenor*
At the Piano : ROMAN MAREK

7. GEORGE & BERT BERNARD
Assisted by GEORGE PIERCE
"Off the Record"

INTERMISSION
Selection from the new American Musical
" Brigadoon "
Played by THE SKYROCKETS ORCHESTRA
under the direction of Woolf Phillips

FULLY LICENCED BARS IN ALL PARTS OF THE THEATRE
Snacks, Teas and Coffee served in the Palm Court

A month after his appearance at the London Palladium Joe received the call to appear at a still more prestigious London venue, the Royal Albert Hall. This concert on 16 May was to have been given by the famous Italian bass-baritone Tito Gobbi, but he was taken ill at the last minute and Joe was brought in as his replacement. In its size and magnificent setting in London's South Kensington, the Albert Hall was quite different from any house Joe had sung in before. The other contributors to the Gobbi concert were already booked: the renowned English-born pianist Marguerite Wolff and Gobbi's original choice of accompanist Ivor Newton.

Wolff was a classically trained musician, who was known for her elegance and glamour. She was said 'to glide on to the concert platform in a jewelled, embroidered creation, with hats, shoes and gloves prepared for each post-concert appearance'. Ivor Newton was equally accomplished in his own way, the favourite accompanist over the years of classical musicians Pablo Casals, Maria Callas and Yehudi Menuhin. Joe might have been excused for feeling intimidated.

However he took it all in his stride, wowing his audience with a mixture of operatic arias and popular Irish songs. He began with 'Macushla', followed by several of his recorded songs: 'Hear My Song, Violetta', 'Come Back to Sorrento', and 'Goodbye' from *The White Horse Inn*. His Irish songs included 'The Garden Where the Praties Grow' and 'The Old House'. Finally there were the arias 'Your Tiny Hand is frozen' from *La Bohème* and 'Take a Pair of Sparking Eyes' from *The Gondoliers*. At the end, he was recalled to the stage three times for encores. Then he sang the two songs from his audition in Belfast: 'I'll Walk beside you' and Gounod's 'Ave Maria'; finishing up with 'Questa o Quella' from Verdi's *Rigoletto*.

After eight long years on the road, Josef Locke had performed in both the London Palladium and the Royal Albert Hall in the space of two months. In terms of his career and popularity, he had finally 'arrived'.

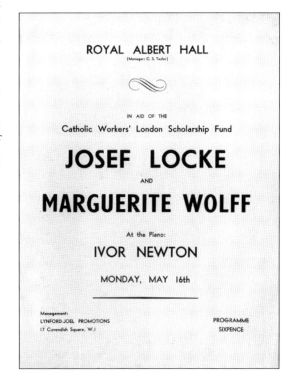

ROYAL ALBERT HALL
(Manager: C. S. Taylor)

IN AID OF THE
Catholic Workers' London Scholarship Fund

JOSEF LOCKE
AND
MARGUERITE WOLFF

At the Piano:
IVOR NEWTON

MONDAY, MAY 16th

Management:
LYNFORD-JOEL PROMOTIONS
17 Cavendish Square, W.I

PROGRAMME
SIXPENCE

Cover of the programme for Joe's first appearance at London's Royal Albert Hall on 16 May 1949. (Author's own collection)

A Family Tragedy

At the end of June 1949, after a brief holiday in Northern Ireland, Joe returned to Blackpool for a three-month run of the *Coconut Grove* revue in the Hippodrome. Although it was advertised as a 'new edition', the mixture was much as before, with the same strong American accent to many of the acts. Jewel and Warriss continued to supply the laughs; the bevy of showgirls, clothed and unclothed, the glamour. Joe gave his by now familiar renderings of popular songs, but there was a newcomer to the programme in the thirteen-year old Julie Andrews, whose variety artist parents were performing along the promenade at the Central Pier.

Joe's and Doreen's second daughter Violetta was born that summer, named from the song that was fast becoming his signature tune. (Her name was shortened to 'Leta' within the family.) But the end of the Blackpool season coincided with a family tragedy, when her sister, two-year old Moira, died unexpectedly on 8 October from a coughing bout brought on by whooping cough. Joe was in Derry at the time, having travelled by boat from Glasgow, thinking his daughter was on the mend. When the news of Moira's death reached him, he immediately caught the ferry back to Glasgow, picked up his car, and drove south to with his stricken wife. Later that week the toddler was buried in Blackpool's Layton Cemetery.

As if to take his mind of their loss, Joe plunged back into a heavy touring schedule, beginning on 22 October with his first appearance on television, as a guest in a new BBC programme *Rooftop Rendezvous*. In the weeks leading up to Christmas he was singing virtually without a break in Peterborough, at the Swansea Empire (where the cast included a new comedy pairing of Eric Morecambe and Ernie Wise), in Glasgow; at the Lewisham Hippodrome, the Finsbury Park Empire, the Birmingham Hippodrome, and the Leeds Empire. Then and only then, perhaps, he was able to spend Christmas at home with Doreen and his baby daughter.

The Josef Locke Album

The publication early in 1950 of *The Josef Locke Album* represented a critical moment in Joe's career. Joe or somebody else – most likely those managing his professional affairs – had decided that he was now famous enough to warrant an 'official' souvenir brochure, with a brief narrative of his life and rise to stardom. The 16-page booklet was part songbook, containing seven of his best known songs arranged for voice and piano accompaniment, and part biography. It had Joe's photograph and endorsement on the front cover with a facsimile of his autograph, and other photographs on the flyleaves and back cover. The story of his life and emergence from obscurity was inaccurate in many of its details and generally glamourized. His arrival in London was put back a year, to 1944, and any mention of May Devitt was 'airbrushed out'. Much was made of John McCormack having acted as mentor to the young Joseph McLaughlin and having advised him that his voice was better suited to the lighter tenor repertoire.

The *Album* was published by Feldman's, the London and Northern England music publishing company, with business connections in Blackpool of course, through 'Feldman's Theatre'. It was to sell hundreds of thousands of copies, at 1/6d a copy. With this new songbook published, three films and several best-selling records under his belt – not to mention his thriving performing career – Joe could look forward to a bright future as the 1950s started.

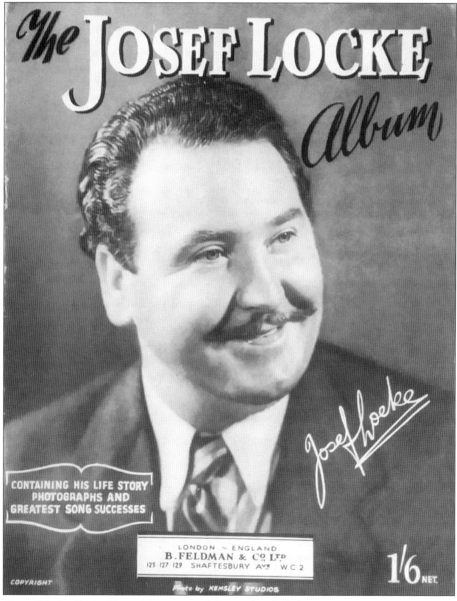

Cover of The Josef Locke Album of sheet music and photographs published in 1950.

CHAPTER FIVE

Winner Takes All
1950-1954

Mr. Blackpool

By the early 1950s Joe was an established variety star throughout the north of England and particularly in Blackpool. The holiday resort's summer revues, showing twice-nightly in various theatres during the season and featuring the leading variety artists and international stars of the day, were one of its main attractions, and Joe one of its chief 'draws'. It earned him the nickname 'Mr. Blackpool', a title he was to share with Reginald Dixon, sometime organist at the Blackpool Tower Ballroom, and half-a-dozen others over the years. Although it is a myth, however often repeated, that he earned it because he topped the bill for nineteen summer seasons in Blackpool, he was a sufficiently regular top-of-the-bill performer in Blackpool summer shows between 1946 and 1954 for the nickname to stick.

It helped fix him in the affections of his northern female fans, of course, that Joe had the looks to go with his marvellous voice. It was later said that he was then "handsome, immaculately tailored and flamboyantly rogueish, with a trim moustache and a twinkling eye for the ladies." And there was his 'Irish charm' too, which Joe could turn on at will, affecting a southern Irish brogue that he, a true son of Derry, had no trace of in his daily speech.

Foreign worlds were opening up for Joe now too. In July 1950 it was reported in the press that an unnamed American promoter had flown to Blackpool to offer him £100,000 for a twelve-month tour of the United States, with an option to renew for a further twelve months – the "biggest ever offer made to an artist to appear in America." Nothing came of this in the short term, but the idea of gaining a new audience in the United States, and even of settling permanently there, lay behind a number of transatlantic trips Joe was to make later in the decade.

The Locke Routine

Joe's pattern of performances through the year was now well established. He was in pantomime from December to January and even early-February; then in variety or revue in the larger northern towns and cities until the start of the summer. Typically the

Joe surrounded by adoring fans in Northern England in the early 1950s.

Joe's own press announcement in summer 1950 that he will be in Blackpool for his 'sixth consecutive season'. (The Stage, 13 July 1950)

July 13, 1950   THE STAGE   29

JOSEF LOCKE

AT THE PIANO - LEN EDWARDS

So happy to be playing my sixth consecutive Blackpool season, and I feel that "SUNNY SERENADE" is the happiest and greatest show of the lot.

I would like to take this opportunity of thanking the B.B.C. for the great compliment paid me of being the only artiste in Blackpool to have a personal programme, which is

"HEAR MY SONG"

A weekly series on the Light Programme each Tuesday evening, commencing July 25th.

Again a big thank you to my good friend Frank Randall for releasing me this summer.

NO VACANCIES TILL 1952

venues were part of the Moss Empire theatre chain in Nottingham, Derby, Hull, Leeds, Newcastle and Sunderland, with whom Joe (through the Grade brothers) had a contractual agreement; but he also appeared regularly in the Empire Theatres north of the border in Glasgow and Edinburgh. The summers, with the partial exception of 1952, he spent in Blackpool rehearsing or performing in some new or revamped revue, spectacular productions designed to appeal to the crowds of holiday-makers. Then in the autumn it was back to touring in variety through the same northern towns and cities until the pantomime season came around again.

Joe's schedule was made heavier by his often taking on extra singing engagements on Sundays when the theatres were closed. We can add to this his recording sessions with Columbia Records, which issued on average five 78 rpm records between 1947 and 1955 – that is, ten new songs – by Joe a year. And in summer 1950, Joe also had his own half-hour weekly radio show *Hear my Song* on the BBC Light Programme, besides occasional other broadcasts. So, we can see how gruelling Joe's workload had become. It was something the *Yorkshire Post* picked up on in an article 'Hard at the Top' which described the singer, in addition to his other commitments, "ploughing his way through a heap of correspondence, comprising both business letters and fan mail," admittedly now with a secretary to help him deal with it. According to entertainer Roy Hudd, his grandmother was one of Joe's biggest fans. She once waited with others at the stage door of her local Empire Theatre hoping to catch a glimpse of her idol, and perhaps even get his autograph. But to her delight Joe flung open the upstairs window of his dressing-room and treated the crowd to an impromptu rendering of 'Hear My Song' and 'I'll Take you home again, Kathleen', before throwing down handfuls of small, signed photographs of himself for them to scramble over.

These small, promotional photos were produced by Columbia, Joe's record company, in the 1950s for Joe to give to his fans at concerts. Both photos above are autographed in Joe's own, distinctive hand-writing which changed little over the years.

1950 was fairly typical. Joe began the year in pantomime, a Jack Taylor production of *Cinderella* at the Theatre Royal, Bolton, which transferred to the Sunderland Empire for a further two-week run ending on 4 February. Later that month he starred in a week's variety show at Belfast's Grand Opera House, and in early March another week in De Montfort Hall in Leicester. And from 20 March until 20 May he was performing without let-up twice-nightly six days a week in a Jack Taylor extravaganza *1001 Marvels* that toured the country from the Moss Empire's flagship, the Finsbury Park Empire, in the south, through the Midlands, to the group's theatres in the north of England and in Scotland. There was a final performance in the Hulme Hippodrome in Manchester on 10 June. Then it was into rehearsal for Henry Hall's revue *Sunny Serenade* which opened in Blackpool's Grand Theatre on 20 June and ran until the middle of September.

How much of a toll this was taking on Joe's health can be gathered from his having to take time off for three weeks in August 1950 suffering from tonsillitis and 'nervous overstrain'. His replacement was singer Ronnie Ronalde who was already performing at another Blackpool theatre. Nightly, it was said, Ronalde had to sprint between 'his theatre' and Joe's, to get his acts done in both shows.

But by October Joe was back performing in *1001 Marvels* again, in the Palace Theatre, Salford, and then back in pantomime in December, in Jack Taylor's *Cinderella* in the Hulme Hippodrome. For the greater part of the autumn, however, he was starring in a series of celebrity concerts organized for him by a young Lancashire impresario J. R. Wyrill Heyworth.

The Heyworth Concerts

Not much is known about Heyworth's background. He was about 29 when he engaged Joe to appear in what was described as 'the most extensive concert tour of this country since the war ended', with over forty cities and towns to be visited. As an impresario he seems to have come from nowhere, without any previous track-record of staging events. His concerts were often on Sunday evenings when the theatres were closed, and the venues were town and city halls, concert and temperance halls. Joe was not his only artist. In the same year that he set up the concerts for Joe, he was also promoting concerts for Issy Bonn, the British-Jewish singer and comedian; for Afrique, the South-African opera singer and mimic; for the singer Lee Lawrence; and George Evans and his orchestra. But his career as an impresario was short-lived and he seems to have severed his connections with show-business by the middle of 1951.

In contrast to the playbills and hoardings used to advertise variety shows, in which the names of all the different acts were piled one on top of the other in a series of boxes, printed in different sizes and colours, Heyworth's advertisements were simple and effective. 'J. R. Wyrill Heyworth Presents' was followed by the name of the star of the show – 'Josef Locke' in this case – placed at the centre in large bold lettering. Presumably, too, this represented for Joe an increased share of the takings, and admission to Heyworth's concerts didn't come cheap: tickets were two or three times the price of variety shows.

No complete list of Joe's Heyworth concerts exists. The first four concerts were on Sundays in spring 1950: in the King's Hall, Derby; the Royal Hall, Harrogate; the Town Hall, Greenock; and the City Hall in Hull. (At this time Joe was already singing during the week in *1001 Marvels*.) There was then a break until the autumn when the tour started up again at the City Hall in Sheffield on 3 November. On this occasion Joe was physically stopped on his way into the building by local members of the Communist Party protesting against a political meeting that was being held inside, but was allowed through when they realized he was Irish and had nothing to do with the meeting.

The high point of the autumn section of the tour was Joe's appearance in London's Royal Albert Hall on 9 November. His fellow performers were soprano Maureen Rose, a protégée of Joe's, and Jimmy Campbell and his orchestra, who were the backing musicians in Joe's weekly *Hear my Song* BBC programme. Joe sang a number of solos – his usual repertoire of popular and

JOSEF LOCKE

A COUNTRY-WIDE AUTUMN CONCERT TOUR

Including the ROYAL ALBERT HALL, London

Exclusively Presented by J. R. WYRILL HEYWORTH

The press announcement in 1950 of Joe's series of concerts for impresario JR Wyrill Heyworth.

PROGRAMME

SAVINGS CONCERT, GUILDHALL, LONDONDERRY
THURSDAY, 7th NOVEMBER, 1946

JOSEPH McLAUGHLIN, World-famous Derry Tenor

Supported by:

Orlando Cafolla, L.T.C.L., M.R.S.T.	-	Violinist
Donald Rowan	- -	Boy Soprano
Cecil Connel	- -	Traditional Singer
Elizabeth Morrison	- - -	Soprano
Wee Willie Doherty	- -	Entertainer
The Londonderriaires	-	Girls' Choir
James Moore, F.T.C.L., A.R.C.O., at the Piano and Organ		

PRICE   -   THREEPENCE

The Programme Cover for Joe's concert in his hometown of Derry in November 1946. He didn't yet use his new stage name of 'Josef Locke' with local audiences, but did describe himself as the 'World Famous Derry Tenor'.

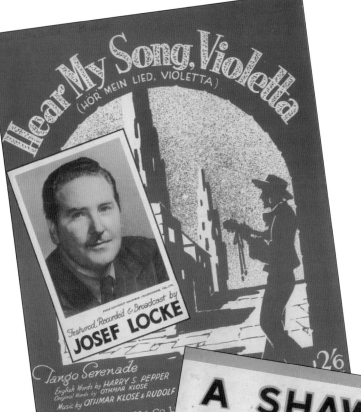

Hear My Song, Violetta
(HÖR MEIN LIED, VIOLETTA)

Featured, Recorded & Broadcast by
JOSEF LOCKE

Tango Serenade
English Words by HARRY S. PEPPER
Original Words by OTHMAR KLOSE
Music by OTHMAR KLOSE & RUDOLF

B. FELDMAN & Co., L
125-9 SHAFTESBURY A' LONDON, W.

2/6

A SHAWL OF GALWAY GREY

BROADCAST & RECORDED BY
JOSEF LOCKE
ON COLUMBIA D.B. 2604

WORDS & MUSIC BY
HAMILTON KENNEDY

BEVAN MUSIC PRODUCTIONS LTD.
SOLE SELLING AGENTS

CAMPBELL, CONNELLY & Co. Ltd., 10 DENMARK STREET, LONDON, WC.2

1/-

Covers of sheet music published in the later 1940s and 1950s when Joe's repertoire had changed from operatic-style melodies to quasi-Irish ballads and love songs. Joe's photos on the front covers were a strong selling-point.

The lively cover of the 1951 Moulin Rouge souvenir programme, the first Blackpool revue in which Joe was a business partner

EDINBURGH
EMPIRE

Chairman PRINCE LITTLER   Managing Director VAL PARNELL
Proprietors - MOSS' EMPIRES, Ltd.   Telephone - 41041.41042
Manager - J. R. HILL

6.25 | Commencing MONDAY, NOVEMBER 19th | 8.40
TWICE NIGHTLY

THE GREAT IRISH TENOR
JOSEF LOCKE

At the Piano: ERNEST BROADBENT

THE INTERNATIONAL MAGICIAN
GALI GALI
Who Scored a Big Success at the
LONDON PALLADIUM

MAUREEN ROSE
THE IRISH NIGHTINGALE

RENÉE DYMOTT
UNUSUAL GIRL

NIXON & DIXON
NEVER A DULL MOMENT

STEWART & MATHEW
PERPETUAL COMMOTION

WALTHON AND DORRAINE
Juggling in the Balance

ROGER CARNE
TELEVISION TOMFOOLERY

MABEL MELROSE SISTERS
IN THE BALANCE

TRIBE BROS., Ltd. London and St. Albans.

A facsimile of the variety bill for Joe's one-week run at the Edinburgh Empire, starting Monday 19 November 1951.

Joe photographed outside Dublin High Court on Monday 7 July 1958, during court proceedings against Matthew Sullivan of Ballybunion. (Irish Photographic Archive).

Joe singing at a Dinner Dance in County Kerry in later November 1958, just a few days after his clandestine departure from Blackpool. (The Kennelly Archive).

Blackpool's Promenade and Tower in the 1950s, a scene Joe would have known well.

Joe, Jimmy O'Dea and his wife, Ursula Doyle photographed at the official opening night of The Ha'Penny Inn on 10 December 1963. (Irish Photographic Archive).

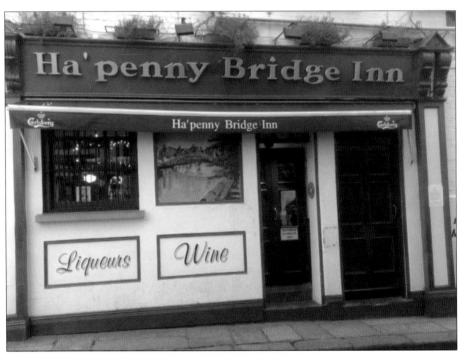

Joe's former pub, The Ha'Penny (Bridge) Inn on Dublin's Wellington Quay as it is today.

The programme cover for Joe's Royal Albert Hall concert on Thursday 9 November 1950, the most prestigious concert in the JR Wyrill Heyworth series.

Royal Albert Hall
Manager: C. S. Taylor

Thursday, November 9th
At 7·30 p.m.

J. R. Wyrill Heyworth

presents

Josef Locke

At the Piano Ernest Broadbent

With
Maureen Rose

Jimmy Campbell
and his Palm Court Orchestra

Irish melodies – with a few operatic arias thrown in for good measure. He also sang three duets with Maureen Rose: two duets from opera and, an oddity, a duet version of the 'Goodbye' song from *The White Horse Inn*. This was one of the first occasions when Joe is reported to have used a microphone, and in the austere view of the *Irish Times* correspondent it made him no better than a 'crooner'.

The series of concerts was continued through November and December in a succession of towns and cities in the Midlands and north of England. There was a lull over the Christmas period and the first three months of 1951, when Joe was in pantomime in Manchester with Frank Randle. The tour was then resumed in April, with two concerts in Northern Ireland: in the Guildhall, in Joe's home town of Derry, and in the Ulster Hall, Belfast. The final concert in the tour was a return visit to the City Hall, Newcastle-upon-Tyne on 13 May 1951.

The Heyworth concerts that we know about fall some way short of the forty-plus concerts originally envisaged. Heyworth was later to charge Joe with having failed to fulfil his part of the contract for other concerts that were to have been held in Wales and the West Country, for which the Burnley-born tenor Ivan Dixon was brought in as substitute. Joe for his part argued that it was only illness – presumably that same tonsillitis and 'nervous overstrain' that had ruled him out of *Sunny Serenade* – that prevented him completing the tour as originally agreed. (In Joe's favour it should be pointed out that on Sunday 20 August he had to cut down his singing, from four songs to two, at a concert in Rhyl, North Wales, owing to being unwell.)

A Second Loss

Joe and Doreen's third daughter was born on Sunday 9 April 1950, but lived for just three days. The couple didn't even have time to give her a name. This, following on from the death of little Moira six months earlier, was a devastating blow. One-year-old Leta remained as Joe and Doreen's only surviving child. But Joe's grieving for the loss of his second daughter didn't prevent him returning to Nottingham the next day to go on with his run at the Empire. If this wasn't literally a case of 'On with the Motley', it was certainly stoicism in the face of personal tragedy.

Doreen's feelings we can only guess at. And perhaps there was a price to be paid by both of them for Joe's seeming determination to go on working regardless. On 1 May, when he was due to begin a week's variety in the Edinburgh Empire, he collapsed with exhaustion and couldn't go onstage. And, as we have seen, the strain of performing night after night told on him later that summer when he had to take a three-week break from the *Sunny Serenade* revue.

Some were to argue later, with the benefit of hindsight, that it was the deaths of the two children within months of one another, Joe's reaction to them, and then his leaving Doreen to grieve alone on both occasions, that caused a rift between them from which the marriage never recovered.

Frank Randle

It cannot have helped that Joe's great friend at this period was the legendary Lancashire comedy actor and carouser Frank Randle. He had been the main man in the Mancunian films that Joe had appeared in in the late 1940s. And he and Joe were to share the stage in the Jack Taylor pantomime *Cinderella* that ran at the Hulme Hippodrome from 23 December 1950 until 17 March 1951. In reality, 'sharing the stage' was precisely what in the course of the run they were reputed *not* to do, as one or other of them often failed to appear for performances. In Randle's case, because he was on a 'bender', but Joe for more complex reasons, not least health ones, but in which drink may have been a factor. Such was the problem hat the management of the Hulme Hippodrome had latterly to promise in advertisements for the pantomime's final weeks that "Josef Locke will definitely appear in each performance."

Together the two revellers, singer and comedian, cut a swathe through the pubs and other watering-holes of the north-west. As Jeff Nuttall puts it in his remarkable book on Randle *King Twist*, "With Locke, the stentorian Irish tenor to whom love descended like a nangellah [?] twice nightly, and Percy Taylor who ran the local taxi-fleet, [Randle] formed a diabolic liaison." They would go out on the town after 10.00 pm when they were through at the theatre and drink the night away. On one particular occasion, "Large quantities of booze turned Randle and Locke, the old firm of iconoclasts, into a couple of whirling dynamos who, in turn, transformed Jimmy Brennan's Lytham hotel, the site of the celebration, into a Mack Sennett set… with caviar dripping down the regency-stripe wallpaper."

Joe enjoying 'a pint' in London in the early 1950s.

Joe could overstep the mark in more innocent ways, as when he insisted on singing nostalgic Irish songs in *The Golden Ball* pub in Poulton-le-Fylde, a favourite spot with Irish seasonal workers employed in the farms nearby, and had to be stopped by the landlord as the pub had no entertainment licence.

There was talk, too, of romantic dalliances in and around Blackpool and of the two men betting and losing large sums of money 'on the horses'. There were card schools late at night behind closed doors with members of Blackpool's Irish mafia. It was stories such as these, of Joe's offstage shenanigans – quite as much as his singing – that lent an air of dash and devilry to his public persona as 'Josef Locke'. None of which can have done much for Doreen, sitting alone at home with her daughter, and seeing little of her husband, even when, as now, he was performing locally and wasn't away on tour.

Illness Strikes Again

Joe had always been drawn to burn the candle at both ends. Quite apart from any carousing and hell-raising, he seems from the very outset of his career to have been driven to take on more and more engagements, in the theatre, on radio and in the recording studio, almost as if he could foresee the time when offers to perform would dry up. Money played a part in it too, of course. As Joe's reputation grew, so also did his expenses and the need to keep working to stay abreast of them. Inevitably the strain told. As early as March 1948 he had collapsed half-way through a song in a *Sing as We Go* broadcast from Belfast, and conductor Douglas Armstrong had to step down from the podium to the microphone and finish the song himself. And while at the London Palladium in April 1949 Joe had to drop out of the show with laryngitis and the Dutch singer Leo Fuld was called up in his place.

However it was in 1950-51 that matters came to a head. The 'indisposition' that kept him from performing on 1 May 1950 at the Edinburgh Empire was followed by a much more serious and prolonged lay-off over the summer. He seemed for a time to recover and was able to go on with the Wyrill Heyworth concerts in the late autumn. But early in March 1951 he was reported as having entered a Manchester nursing home suffering from a nervous breakdown. "I have cancelled all my radio and stage contracts," he told the Irish News Agency: "Overwork has brought about this trouble. I have been singing too many songs seven days a week." Much was made in the press of the fact that his illness was costing him £800 a week in lost engagements and the cancellation of a planned American tour that was to have earned him £100,000.

This was Joe's third and most serious brush with illness in twelve months, and he seems to have taken the advice of his doctor and kept his engagements over the next three months to a minimum.

Meanwhile at the *Moulin Rouge*

Rehearsals for the new Blackpool revue *Moulin Rouge* began in June 1951, and for the first time ever Joe was not just performing in the show. Through his theatrical agency Josef Locke Ltd, he had negotiated with Tom Arnold and Jack Taylor to be their business partner. The change was signalled on the front page of the revue programme: 'In Association with Josef Locke Ltd'. But in case no one had noticed, Joe took out a half-page advertisement in *The Performer*, the trade journal of the variety world, headed by a flattering photograph of himself and his name in large letters, which said that he was happy to be the partner of the two older impresarios, and to be co-starring in the show with his friend Vic Oliver.

Moulin Rouge opened in Blackpool's Hippodrome on Saturday 30 June. As one might guess from the name, it drew inspiration from the racier aspects of Parisian night-life, and had scenes called 'Arc de Triomphe' and 'Montmartre'. There was a chorus line of dancing girls wearing not very much whose high-kicking delighted the audiences and was a passable imitation of the dancers at the original *Moulin Rouge* in Paris. The *Belle Époque* theme of the show was not done to death however. There were other scenes, 'A Little Bit of Lancashire' and 'Tchaikovsky Fantasia', which could have featured in any one of a dozen Blackpool revues down the years.

Each new Arnold-Taylor revue in the early 1950s cost around £17,000 to produce, roughly £500,000 in today's money. So too with *Moulin Rouge*. No expense was spared, on the costumes – what there was of them – on the scenery, on the choreography and on the staging. It must have cost Joe as joint-promoter a pretty penny, which he would have reckoned to get back from the takings.

His own performing contributions to the show came in the opening 'Arc de

Programme cover of the 1951 Moulin Rouge revue showing Joe's first foray into business partnership in Blackpool.

Joe's announcement of his new business partnership in the Moulin Rouge revue in Blackpool's Hippodrome in summer 1951. (The Performer, 19 July 1951)

Triomphe' scene and in section fourteen, 'Selections in Song'. That Joe had a financial interest in the revue's success must, one would think, have been an incentive for him to 'go for broke' in his own vocal solos. And perhaps it was. But he was forced to miss one performance in the last week of the run, when recurring breathing difficulties persuaded him to see a Manchester specialist for a chest X-ray, his fourth bout of illness in two years.

Betty Barr

By summer 1951 Joe had met Elizabeth Barr, a leggy twenty-year old model, known as 'Betty', and was soon head over heels in love with her. They had met in England, where Betty had lived most of her life, although she was born in County Fermanagh. Unlike other women with whom Joe had had casual relationships, she was set on marrying Joe, and the only question was how this was to be achieved.

Except by surmise we know next to nothing about Joe's relations with Doreen at this time, but it was she who made the first move, petitioning for divorce on grounds of cruelty and adultery. The case was heard on Thursday 29 November 1951 in a Manchester courtroom. Joe, who was then starring in variety in Glasgow, travelled down by train for the proceedings, accompanied by a 'tall and attractive blonde'. In court Joe's barrister submitted the surprise counter-claim that the marriage to Doreen had never been valid, since it had taken place four months before his divorce from Essie, his first wife, had been made absolute.

Thus the haste with which Joe and Doreen had been married in 1947, following the decree *nisi* in the Belfast court, went against her in a legal sense. The judge had no option but to rule that the marriage between Joe and Doreen was null and void; and that therefore Doreen's petition for divorce from Joe on grounds of cruelty and adultery had no standing in law. But he was clearly sympathetic to Doreen's plight, which he described as 'a great misfortune'; and, in accepting Joe's barrister's submission, he did so with the proviso that Joe pay Doreen £6,000 in compensation plus all the legal costs.

Joe, all things considered, was let off lightly, the judge commenting only that he should have exercised more care in his 'marital arrangements'.

So in a matter of hours Joe's four-year old 'marriage' to Doreen was over, and he didn't even have to wait for a decree absolute before he was free to marry again. Less than seven weeks later, Joe and Betty were married – this time, legally – in Marylebone Registry Office in London on 16 January 1952. They had but a short time together before Joe was off on his travels again, on a variety tour of Canada with the Cockney comedian Tommy Trinder. It was Joe's first overseas tour, and his first trip abroad since his days in the Irish Guards.

The First Overseas Tour

Joe and Trinder left London by train on 30 January, travelling to Liverpool from where they took ship to St John's, New Brunswick. Their touring show was called *Music Hall Varieties*, with Trinder – billed as 'Britain's No.1 Comedian' – the main attraction. However Joe's name was almost as prominent on the advertisements, his fame as a recording artist and as 'The Great Irish Tenor' having preceded him. The support acts included the Canadian dance team of Alan and Blanche Lund; Ray Overbury, a novelty musician and dancer; the juggler and slack-rope artist Jose Moreno; and the Elkins sisters, gymnasts and contortionists. The Variety Club of Toronto sponsored the tour to raise funds for their vocational school for disabled children.

The show opened in Toronto's Royal Alexandra Theatre on 11 February for four nights, toured to various towns and cities in Ontario in the following week, and went on to Ottawa and Montreal. The company then took the train westwards to Manitoba (Winnipeg and Brandon), Saskatchewan (Regina and Saskatoon) and Alberta (Edmonton and Calgary). Originally the tour was to have ended in Vancouver and Victoria in British Columbia, but by popular demand it was extended by a week for closing performances in Toronto in April. There were almost forty performances over the eight weeks.

Apart from initial problems with the public-address system the first night in Toronto, Joe's singing was warmly received by his Canadian audiences: "[He] has a wonderful voice… well balanced repertoire"; "had his audience enthusiastically requesting

An advert in the Canadian press for one of
Joe and Tommy Trinder's shows in 1952.
(Toronto Daily Star, 9 February 1952)

favourite songs", "had the audience won before he sang a note", "a sweet voice and an ingratiating way with the audience"; "Mr Locke proved himself to be a sensitive artist as well as an admirable showman." Joe could be well satisfied with how his first overseas tour had gone.

The tour party arrived back in England on 14 April 1952. Within a week, rested and rejuvenated from the long sea voyage, Joe plunged into a punishing round of appearances at the various theatres of the Moss Empire chain that took him almost without a break until the end of August. His appearances in Blackpool were restricted to a week in *Palace Varieties* at the Palace Theatre, the first time since 1946 that he had not been booked for the full season in a Blackpool summer revue – a consequence perhaps of his being out of the country in the early part of year when bookings for the summer were being finalized.

Domestic Matters

In August 1952 Joe purchased a large detached two-storey house in Lytham St Annes, his largest and most expensive property to date. It was called *Cintra* and sat on the Inner Promenade at Fairhaven, looking out over the Irish Sea. It was set in its own grounds and built of 'warm red Accrington brick', with a huge roof of Westmoreland green slate. It cost Joe around £7,000.

As for the interior, there was a stunning dining-hall 'clad in burr walnut', with lamps built in to the newel posts at the foot of the stairs, an art deco bathroom of green, black and gold tiling with a bell push that could be pressed for service from the bath itself, a large drawing–room ideal for after-show entertaining, and five large bedrooms. Throughout it was furnished in an art deco style with a level of opulence befitting a star of Joe's reputation and wealth.

Shortly after Joe and Betty moved into their new home, she gave birth to a baby boy, Joseph. It was Joe's first son, after four daughters in succession.

The First Royal Variety Performance

On 3 November 1952 Joe was able to tick off another first in his career when he appeared in front of the young Queen Elizabeth in her first Royal Variety Performance at the London Palladium. Among those taking part on this occasion were the singers Gracie Fields and Vera Lynn; the pianist Winifred Atwell and Reginald Dixon (Joe's rival for the title of 'Mr. Blackpool'). Among the comedians were Arthur Askey, Jimmy Edwards and Max Bygraves. There were foreign guests, too, in Maurice Chevalier and Joe's fellow tenor, the Italian Beniamino Gigli. Joe's contribution to the programme was to sing 'The Isle of Innisfree', the theme tune of that year's Oscar-winning film, *The Quiet Man*, starring John Wayne and the Irish actress Maureen O'Hara.

Joe's appearance at the Royal Variety Performance was something of an interlude in his otherwise very full schedule of engagements that autumn that took him from Derby to Peterborough, to Belfast, to Wolverhampton, Leeds and Liverpool. Over Christmas and New Year he was Baron Hardup in *Cinderella* at the Oldham Empire. The pulling power of his name was such by this time that he was able to stipulate that he shouldn't have any dialogue or be required to act – not Joe's strengths, admittedly – but that it should be enough for him to come onstage, sing his numbers, and then go off for the rest of the show.

It was while Joe was performing in Oldham that he was seen in Ashton-under-Lyne by a young boy for whom it was still a cherished memory half a century later. It was a Sunday and 'this large handsome fellow with a black moustache' emerged from a pub escorted by a large crowd 'most carrying pints with them'. He was wearing a black overcoat and black Homberg hat. "He mounted a pile of rubble and concrete, and I'll never forget till my dying day as he broke into song. He sang *Jerusalem*, his fine voice amplified by the brick and concrete amphitheatre (of the surrounding buildings). There were many grown men crying their eyes out, I can tell you." It was only later that the boy learned that the singer was Josef Locke.

It's a revealing story. Joe never could turn down an invitation to sing. It didn't matter that he wasn't being paid, or that it was in the back room of a pub, or, as in this case, on a patch of rough ground outside. If people genuinely wanted to hear him sing, he would give of his best, and then, by the way he clearly felt the words of the song move them to tears.

Something of this gift of being able to enthral an audience was seen when Joe appeared in Derry on 22 January 1953 in a concert in aid of Derry City Football Club. It was, the press said, an 'all-Derry night', with the exception of Ernest Broadbent, Joe's accompanist. Others performing were James MacCafferty's all-male ensemble 'The Ten Columbians' and young bass singer Willie Loughlin. But it was Joe, singing over a dozen songs, both solos and duets, who 'made the atmosphere in the Guildhall more

Joe's father, Patrick McLaughlin (1875-1960) pictured in his later years when he was living at his son Thomas's home, 8 Artillery Street, Derry.

like an informal party'. In the most moving moment of the night Joe called attention to the presence in the audience of his elderly father Patrick – now retired to Derry – and the old man was warmly applauded.[1]

Sale of Cintra

Then suddenly, on his return to Blackpool – and just six months after moving into *Cintra*, the couple's splendid new home – Joe put the house up for sale. It was bought by George Formby and his wife Beryl for £1,000 less than Joe had paid for it the previous summer. The fact that he sold it so soon after buying it and was prepared to take a loss on the transaction suggests that he was, if only temporarily, strapped for cash. Joe himself later told a journalist that he sold the house to free up money to pay his income-tax arrears. But it was known at the time that he had recently bought a riding school in the area, and it may have been buying the riding school that over-stretched his finances. Joe always seems to have lived up to his income of the moment and it wouldn't be surprising if he sometimes got his sums wrong.

Whatever lay behind the sale, Formby and wife moved into the house which they promptly renamed *Beryldene*, and were to live there until George's death in 1961. Meanwhile Betty and Joe with young Joseph moved to a more modest house at 150 St Annes Road East, St Annes-on-Sea. It must have been something of a come-down for Betty and, if she were the worrying sort, a worrying portent of how things might go in the future.

Singing in the Reign

Throughout spring 1953 Joe continued to appear in variety shows around the country, but was also caught up in planning for Blackpool's new season. And in this 'special' summer he formed a partnership with his friend Jimmy Brennan bring out a revue to celebrate the coronation of the new Queen. (Brennan had just bought and renovated what was previously Feldman's Theatre, and renamed it the 'Queen's Theatre'.) Their

---

[1] *Joe's father, Patrick McLaughlin died seven years later, in June 1960. He and his wife, Annie (died 1971) are buried together in Derry City Cemetery.*

Joe captured in typical full flow at one of his concerts, his eyes bright, his arms outstretched.

QUEEN'S
THEATRE

Tel.: 21048   Tel.: 21048

Proprietors: J. B. R. Cinemas (Alexandra) Ltd.

Licensee .... James Brennan
Resident Manager .... Edward Forshaw
Assistant Manager .... Dennis Chritchley
Musical Director .... Dennis Seener
Stage Manager .... Alec. Peters
Electrician .... Wilf Powell

6-15 — TWICE NIGHTLY — 8-40

Prices of Admission:

Orch. Stalls & **6/-** | Stalls & **5/-** | Back Stalls & **4/-** | Side **3/-**
Grand Circle | Circle | Back Circle | Stalls

Including Tax.   Bookable in Advance

JAMES BRENNAN and JOSEF LOCKE Present
Their Coronation Season Production

"Singing in the Reign"

Devised, Produced and Staged by
HARRY BRIGHT
with Choreography by MAUREEN SIMS

RULES AND REGULATIONS
(In accordance with the requirements of the Blackpool Corporation)

(a) The Public may leave at the end of the performance by all exits and entrances other than those used as queue waiting-rooms, and the doors of such exits and entrances shall at that time be open.

(b) All gangways, passages and staircases shall be kept entirely free from chairs or any other obstructions.

(c) Persons shall not be permitted to stand or sit in any of the intersecting gangways. If standing be permitted at the rear of the seating, sufficient space shall be left for persons to pass easily to and fro.

(d) The safety curtain shall at all times be maintained in working order and shall be lowered at the beginning of and during the time of every performance.

Another 'Josef Locke' co-production, Singing in the Reign in Blackpool's Queen's Theatre in summer 1953. (Author's own collection)

revue, echoing the 1952 film starring Gene Kelly and Cyd Charisse, was given the punning title of *Singing in the Reign*.

It ran right through the summer months from 25 May to 17 October, an unusually long summer season for a Blackpool show, but Brennan and Joe probably reckoned the extra weeks would give them their best chance of recouping their investment. For the cast, apart from Joe himself topping the bill, there was Nat Jackley, a comedian who had built a career in comedy out of having a rubber-neck and 'educated' legs; his then wife, the dancer Marianne Lincoln; the Musical Elliotts, a trio of concertina players; and the usual corps de ballet of Blackpool lovelies. Its opening chorus of 'Blackpool Wonderful Blackpool' was a celebration of the town and its visitors.

Joe was, as ever, the astute businessman and arranger of clever photo opportunities. While the revue was running he arranged to have the shapely Marianne Lincoln photographed by *Picture Post* relaxing on a horse from his own stables, and in that way advertised both the stables and the summer show they were both appearing in.

We don't know if Joe made a profit from his investment in the revue. Perhaps not, since he never again risked his own money in this way. In any case he had, besides his stables and riding school, other irons in the fire. There was his theatrical agency. And around this time he also had a garage-cum-car-showroom, 'Josef Locke Motors (Blackpool) Ltd', in Whitegate Drive, which supplied top-of-the-range American cars, mainly to his fellow-performers. It was hinted that Joe had an arrangement with a Dublin car dealer to supply him with these cars which couldn't be imported directly into England in the post-war years. The cars were registered as second-hand, which made it legal to import them, although they were only second-hand in the sense of having been driven around for a hundred miles or so in Ireland, before being shipped to England.

On the Airwaves

By 1953 Joe was a seasoned performer on radio. He was regularly heard live on the BBC Light Programme and the Home Service and his records often played on air. His records were also played on Radio Éireann, although he had not given a concert in the

Republic of Ireland for at least eight years – not since his departure in 1945. He had also appeared a handful of times on television. But on 30 May, just three days before the Queen's Coronation, he was one of a number of stars in variety – Mantovani, Winifred Atwell, Billy Cotton and Victoria Campbell – who appeared in a major live television broadcast *Coronation Music Hall* from the Empire Theatre in London. Coming so soon after his appearance at the *Royal Variety Performance* the previous autumn, it confirmed Joe's place among the elite of the entertainment world.

But it didn't make him immune to criticism. Some months after the Coronation broadcast, on 22 November 1953, Joe was in a radio broadcast from 'his hometown of Londonderry', one of Terry-Thomas's *Top of the Town* series on the BBC Light Programme. Calling it 'Londonderry' was bad enough for a Derry Catholic. But an irate *Irish Press* reviewer Julia Monks found the whole programme vulgar and insulting, the worst sort BBC 'Oirish' stereotype, with its "leprechauns, spalpeens, colleens and all the rest of the preposterous paraphernalia – Locke, stock and barrel, as you might say… Mr. Locke should feel heartily ashamed at having taken part in it." She invited suggestions from readers – doubtless tongue in cheek – about how Radio Éireann might retaliate.

An Arm and a Throat

While starring in the pantomime *Aladdin* at the Wolverhampton Hippodrome in January 1954 Joe fell down a stairway while on stage and broke his arm. Perhaps this

Joe is his 'recording heyday' photographed in a typical session.

was the 'indisposition' that led to him being replaced for the remainder of the run by 'the great Frederick Ferrari, Radio's Favourite Singing Star.' But he may also have been having trouble with his throat. He was later to say that he had an urgent throat operation in early 1954, so perhaps he took the injury to his arm and the resulting enforced lay-off from work as an opportunity to have a surgeon look at what must have been an already existing throat condition. What the problem was, what kind of operation it was, and where it was carried out, we don't know, but Joe – ever the horse-betting man – said that his medical bills for the treatment came to '650 guineas'.

He certainly wasn't off work for long. By mid-February he was back on tour again, clocking up the miles and the nightly appearances in variety. In late March, however, in a major departure from his usual routine he collected Betty and his baby son Joseph and the three of them left for the United States. We know almost nothing about this first American trip beyond what can be gathered from a Newcastle Empire playbill of 12 April that referred to his having come 'Direct from his American Tour' and a report in *The Stage* magazine of 15 April that said he was "just returned from America, where he sang in concerts at Las Vegas, New York and Hollywood, and was screen-tested for the film of John McCormick's [sic] life." Interesting information if true, but, unlike his earlier tour of Canada, it hasn't yet been possible to confirm any of these details from newspapers or sources closer to the events in the United States itself.

A Welcome to Her Majesty

Shortly after his return from America Joe was involved in a major 'live' television broadcast, *Celebration Music Hall*, a variety show from the BBC Television Studio in London on 15 May 1954, to welcome home the Queen and Prince Philip from their six-month Commonwealth Tour in the royal yacht *Britannia*. It was introduced by Terry-Thomas and, apart from Joe, featured a number of prominent show-business figures: Billy Cotton and his Band, Nat Jackley, Leslie ('Hutch') Hutchinson, The Television Toppers and the Band of the Coldstream Guards.

For the rest of 1954 Joe was on tour with his accompanist Ernest Broadbent, crisscrossing the country from the Theatre Royal in Portsmouth to the Edinburgh Empire, and from Cardiff's New Theatre to the Bradford Alhambra. Unlike previous years, he wasn't in any of the long-running Blackpool summer shows, but he had a week in *Palace Varieties* at Blackpool's Palace Theatre at the beginning of June and another week in early September. In August he and Broadbent were due to give two concerts in the Guildhall in Derry, but Joe was 'indisposed' – that catch-all for the different health problems that dogged him around this time – and the concerts had to be cancelled. The advertisement for the concerts had claimed "after a highly successful coast-to-coast tour of America."

Joe ended the year in pantomime with Frank Randle again, this time in *Aladdin* at the Theatre Royal, Bolton.

Joe and Betty Barr, photographed arriving in Dublin Airport, then Collinstown Airport, in March 1955, with their son Joseph. By then, the couple had been married just over three years. (Irish Photographic Archive)

CHAPTER SIX

The Gathering Storm
1955-1958

The Transatlantic Traveller

Joe travelled to America again in mid-April 1955, the second of at least six such trips he was to make in the next five years. These visits, which took him to east and west coasts and points in-between, were time spent away from his singing career in England, without doing much to establish a new career and reputation for himself as a singer across the Atlantic. In truth they were less about Joe 'chasing the American Dream' than they were about him trying to keep his marriage to Betty alive; and then, when that failed, trying to extricate himself from it with the least collateral damage. Inevitably, however, as the couple's relationship deteriorated into rows and recrimination, it was their son, young Joseph who was often the pawn.

Round about this time Joe began to turn his eyes towards Ireland again, to re-establish his career there. He got in touch with many of his old showbusiness friends in Dublin and elsewhere, returning to sing on stages he had last appeared on over a decade before. And he spent two long summers in the west of Ireland, eschewing the variety shows of his heyday to sing at dances in the new ballrooms that were springing up everywhere. There was a succession of high profile court cases, a new woman in his life, and mounting difficulties over his tax affairs. So that, although up to the mid-1950s things had seemed, professionally speaking, to be going Joe's way, he was entering a more unsettled period of his career, when his seemingly smooth and irresistible rise to the top was to receive its first check.

Return of the Native

Towards the end of March 1955, in a surprise move, Joe returned to sing in Dublin for the first time in almost ten years, doing a week's run in his old stomping ground, the Theatre Royal. Louis Elliman, manager at the Royal, had begun a month's trial of a show, *All Star Variety* to see if the Theatre's waning fortunes could be revived. Joe starred in the fourth week of the run, following Dickie Valentine, Bonar Colleano, and Billy Cotton and his Band. Elliman was an old friend and Joe may have been doing him a favour in agreeing to appear.

The *Irish Independent* reminisced that it had been thirteen years since Joe had last appeared on that stage, and then only as 'a down-the-bill turn'. "The intervening years," it went on, "had added to his stature as a singer and a stage personality." Certainly Joe drew a larger audience than any of the previous lead artists, the newspaper explaining that this was, "not because he was an Irishman", but because he was "equally good when singing 'straight' or when 'crooning'." He got a particularly warm reception for his 'Soldier's Dream' and 'Sorrento'.

This run was the beginning of the second phase of Joe's career in Ireland, when he divided his time more or less equally between Ireland and England. Being back in Ireland must, surely, have reminded him of his fledgling days on the Dublin stage when he was just starting to make a name for himself. And perhaps he was struck anew by the affection Irish audiences felt for him as one of their own. Joe was later to confide to a journalist that in England he had often felt himself to be surrounded by 'hangers-on, cadgers and spongers', many of whom owed him considerable sums of money, and how it was a relief to get away. Over the next few years he was increasingly to spend time in Ireland and to use its ports and airports as starting points for his visits to America.

However Joe returned to Blackpool from Dublin on 4 April for a week's run in *Palace Varieties* at the Palace Theatre, in time for the Eastertime crowds. Among the supporting acts was a young comedian Terry Scott, who was just starting out on a career in show-business. In Joe's absence, his friend, comedian Danny Cummins, scored a hit at the Theatre Royal when he did his impersonation of 'Josef Locke', a take-off of Joe's most characteristic mannerisms. Apparently Joe took it all in good part.

THEATRE ROYAL, DUBLIN

WEEK OF MARCH 28th, 1955

1. OVERTURE — Jimmy Campbell and the Theatre Royal Orchestra	10. THE ROYALETTES — Scottish Journey
2. THE ROYALETTES — On with the Show	11. DOROTHY REID & MAC — To Entertain Again
3. THE TWO ANGELOS — Young Aerialists	12. ROB MURRAY — The International Humourist
4. DOROTHY REID & MAC — Accordionists	
5. DESMOND & MARKS — Fooling and Falling	13. **JOSEF LOCKE**
6. THE ROYALETTES — "Hot Toddy"	ERNEST BROADBENT
7. JACK "RECORD ROUND UP" JACKSON — Famous Disc Jockey	at the Piano
8. WILSON, KEPPEL & BETTY — "Cleopatra's Nightmare"	
	FULLY LICENSED BARS ON ALL FLOORS
9. INTERVAL — Singing with Tommy Dando	Ices, Fruit Drinks, Popcorn, Chocolates and Cigarettes available from Attendants

The programme for Joe's week at the Theatre Royal in March-April 1955, his first appearance in Dublin for almost ten years. (Author's own collection)

74

For your greater pleasure Josef Locke records exclusively on

COLUMBIA

Here is a comprehensive list of his recordings:

IDB33	Come back to Sorrento. Santa Lucia.		
IDB36	My Heart and I. Goodbye.		
IDB40	Hear my song, Violetta. I'll take you home again, Kathleen.		
IDB84	Dear Old Donegal. The Rose of Tralee.		
IDB90	Ave Maria (Gounod). The Rosary.	IDB360	To-night Beloved. Charmaine.
IDB91	Galway Bay. Macushla.	IDB390	Isle of Innisfree. Mother Machree.
IDB102	Hush-a-bye Rose of Killarney. The old Bog Road.	IDB430	One Little Candle. Wonderful Copenhagen.
IDB116	Bless this house. Song of Songs.	IDB472	Tobermory Bay. Shades of Old Blarney.
IDB125	When the Angelus was Ringing. The Soldier's Dream.	IDB481	The Rose of Slievenamon. The Bard of Armagh.
IDB130	Beneath Thy Window. Toselli's Serenade.	IDB520	You're just a flower from an old Bouquet A Kiss, a Smile and a Tear.
IDB189	Christopher Robin is Saying His Prayers. The Story of the Sparrows	IDB521	Cara Mia. When it's Moonlight in Mayo.
IDB192	The Garden Where the Praties Grow. Eileen O'Grady.	IDB526	In the Chapel in the Moonlight. Drinking Song "Student Prince"
IDB222	Teddy Bear's Picnic If I were a Blackbird.	IDB537	Santa Natale. Maire, My Girl.
IDB229	When You Talk about Old Ireland If I can Help Somebody.	IDX29	Holy City. Star of Bethlethem.
IDB245	You are my Heart's Delight March of the Grenadiers.	IDX87	Take a Pair of Sparkling Eyes. Nirvana.

The Artists'

Choice— **COLUMBIA**

Issued by the Gramophone Company Limited, 35 Parliament Street, Dublin

By 1955 Joe had racked up an impressive number of recordings, as shown by this advert in a Dublin theatre programme in April that year. (Author's own collection)

Without the Royal Command

What Joe did not take in good part – or so it was said – was his omission from the line-up for the 1955 Royal Command Performance in Blackpool's Opera House. Impresario Jack Hylton had pulled off a rare coup in getting the prestigious event staged there on 13 April, the first time it had ever been held outside London.

Given his standing in Blackpool around this time, Joe could well have expected to be one of the first names on the cast-list, so his chagrin at being passed over would be understandable. How he came to be left out, when so many of his friends and fellow performers, among them George Formby and Jewel and Warriss, were included, is perplexing. Jack Hylton, after all, was the man who first gave Joe his chance in July 1945. Were there others behind the scenes in Blackpool whom Joe had offended in some way? Was it Val Parnell's revenge? Whatever the reason, Joe decided not to hang about but to take himself off to America instead.

Visits to America

On this, Joe's second American trip, he was accompanied by Betty and son Joseph. They flew first of all to New York, and then onwards to California. As on his first trip, we know almost nothing about any bookings he may have had, with one exception: a report in a Californian newspaper of 20 April 1955 that he was signed up for a six-week engagement at Las Vegas. There were presumably other bookings, since later that year, when he was back performing in Belfast, he was advertised as coming 'Direct from his Record-Breaking American Tour', which can hardly refer to this single engagement in Las Vegas. Or so one would think, unless we are to take it as an extreme example of advertising hype.

By his own admission Joe didn't enjoy his time in America. He was often bored. "I couldn't stand being in California at all… I used to lie about in the sun at Long Beach day after day with nothing to do. It was dreadful." Coming to America hadn't been his idea, but Betty's. "A man's wife wants him to do something or to buy something and you start by saying no and finish by saying yes;" adding ruefully, "Tis the way things have always been with me." As for his time in Las Vegas, he found the audiences in the casinos noisy and inattentive, basically because the drinks were free and they drank a lot. "As I told people at the time, audiences didn't stay quiet for Frank Sinatra, so what bloody chance had I got?"

Joe was back in England by the middle of June 1955 where he did a week at the Theatre Royal in Portsmouth, then a week in a "Holiday Variety Show" in Belfast's Grand Opera House. Joe proudly announced in the programme that he was arriving back "Direct from his Record Breaking American Tour". Young Joseph had returned with his father, while Betty had decided to stay on in California, hoping to take up a career in modelling.

However within a few months, in November 1955, Joe had flown back to America to arrange dates for a 'coast to coast' concert and TV tour. This took place in March

Our Holiday Variety Show

WEEK COMMENCING JULY 11th, 1955

1. OVERTURE

2. ROLYS and PARTNER...Juggler on the Roller

3. PETER and SAM SHERRY
   The Versatile Brothers

4. DUO RUSSMAR................Beauty in Balance

5. EDDIE ARNOLD..................Mr. Everybody

6. INTERMISSION
   By Grand Opera House Orchestra
   Conducted by Tom Cooney

7. LES HELLVOS......................Aerial Thrills

8. BILLY MAXAM...........Television's Newsboy

9. # JOSEF LOCKE
   Direct from his Record Breaking
   American Tour

   (At the Piano—WILL FYFFE, Junr.)

The programme for Joe's week in 'Our Holiday Variety Show' at Belfast's Grand Opera House in mid-July 1955. The following week he was singing in the Bournemouth Pavilion, appearing alongside Peter Sellers and Spike Milligan.

of the following year. Joe flew into New York at the beginning of the month and was photographed on the steps of the plane being presented with a gift by a TWA stewardess. He was booked to sing in Chicago and Boston, before returning to New York for his debut appearance in the city's Carnegie Hall on 23 March 1956 – not quite the 'coast to coast' tour promised, but still a recital at America's premier concert venue. He was joined in the concert by Limerick soprano Mona Geary and Joseph Rankin, who played selections on the xylophone. Reviewing the concert, the *New York Times* described his voice as of "striking natural beauty, especially in its upper-middle range", although it detected some straining on the top notes and regretted his use of a microphone "which made it hard for people who like to hear voices as they really are." His programme was made up chiefly of Irish popular songs and ballads put over with that shameless appeal to sentiment in his audience that was Joe's hallmark.

It was while Joe was in New York on this trip that there was an incident involving him and 'New York's Finest'. According to Joe Lynch who told the story, Joe and Betty with Joe Lynch were being driven through Central Park late at night by their friend Joe Rizzo, a wealthy New York businessman. Rizzo failed to come to a complete halt at one of the intersections and was waved down by two policemen. Rizzo did the usual thing for a New Yorker in these circumstances and handed over his driving-licence with a ten dollar bill. But when Joe (Locke) saw this, he flew into a rage, accused the men of taking bribes, and told them that when he was a policeman he would never have done such a thing. It was the only time, Lynch said, that he ever saw Joe completely lose the rag. It ended up with Joe Rizzo having to fork out another 200 dollars to placate the by-now thoroughly incensed pair of cops who were all set to arrest the singer and give him a night in the cells.

Joe was to make later trips to the U.S., as we will see, but this 1956 visit and his Carnegie Hall concert probably represented the highpoint of his career there. Compared with the success achieved in America by other Irish singers – not just John McCormack, but Joe's fellow townsman Michael O'Duffy, and others such as Brendan O'Dowda – it was all rather underwhelming. Summing up his experience of America in general, Joe was later to say (in a moment of candour) to journalist Douglas Enefer: "Let's face it. I didn't do anything big there."

Irish Summers

The two summers following this 1956 trip to America Joe spent in the rural quiet of the west of Ireland. From the second half of April 1956 he was staying with a friend Matthew Sullivan in County Kerry. Sullivan had just bought the Central Hotel in Ballybunion and had added on a superb new ballroom, so Joe and he hatched a plan to launch the ballroom in spectacular style. Joe had no bookings in Blackpool for that 1956 season, so he readily agreed to sing at the opening night and for some weeks thereafter. The event was publicized well in advance. Lengthy articles appeared in the local press describing the size, fittings and up-to-the-minute sound equipment of the new building. The amplification and acoustics were claimed to be the finest of any ballroom in the land. A plane-load of expatriate Irishmen and women was expected from London and several American-Irish groups from New York for the opening night. Joe, billed as 'direct from the Carnegie Hall, New York', was to do the honours on this occasion, his 'special and only engagement in Ireland'.

It was 11.00pm on 29 June 1956 when Joe made his entrance to declare the ballroom 'officially' open. It had been packed to capacity from early evening, with further hundreds, who had come for the opening night, left disappointed outside. Those lucky to be inside were treated to half-an-hour of Joe singing from his usual repertoire – to great applause and cheering – followed by duets with soprano Mollie Millar.

Joe stayed for several more weeks – in fact, for the rest of that summer – free of charge at Sullivan's hotel in Ballybunion. There he was able to relax in pleasant surroundings by the sea, play the occasional round of golf, and have his meals with wine provided for him. In exchange – according to Sullivan – he was to sing once a week or more in the new ballroom. This informal arrangement didn't stop Joe also singing, of his own accord and without charging a fee, in local pubs. Joseph spent part of the summer with his father in Ballybunion, but then flew to California to be with his mother, with Sullivan paying his airfare.

Local newspapers carried several interviews with Joe around this time. In one piece he was said to be 'almost a local here now', because of the amount of time he was spending in the Ballybunion area. Joe was to buy a large four-bedroomed house *Sea Cliff* overlooking Ballybunion Strand. It had two reception rooms, a dining room and four bedrooms with a south-facing glass verandah. Most importantly from Joe's point of view, it was within easy reach of the local golf course. In addition, Joe had recently made another purchase, a 1,000 acre farm in County Meath, having previously sold his home in Blackpool while he was in America. All the signs were that Joe was in the process of divesting himself of his properties in England and intending to make Ireland his future base.

But with summer in Ballybunion over, Joe was drawn once more to America in mid-September, when he went to collect Joseph from Betty in California and bring him back to Ireland. He was there for the best part of two months, ostensibly 'an American tour', if reports in Irish newspapers are to be believed – but again there are no details or confirmation from newspapers or other sources on the American side.[1]

Father and son travelled back to Ireland by ship, docking in Cobh Harbour on 9 November 1956. Young Joseph was now four years old, so Joe decided to send him to the Christian Brothers' School in Dublin's Westland Row.

There is no record of Joe performing anywhere in winter 1956-57, nor do we know where he spent the winter months. The likelihood is that he was resting up, either in Dublin or at his new farm in County Meath. Either way, he emerged from his possibly

---

[1] *There was a bizarre offshoot to this fifth American trip. On 31 October the Irish Press carried a story that Joe had cabled Matthew Sullivan from New York to say that his wife Betty had been killed in a car crash in California two days earlier. It proved to be false alarm, but whether there was an accident and Betty injured in it, we don't know.*

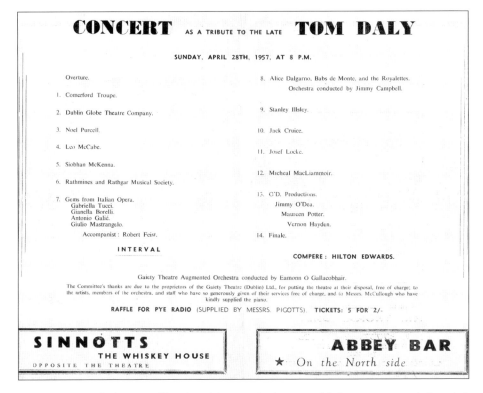

CONCERT AS A TRIBUTE TO THE LATE TOM DALY

SUNDAY, APRIL 28TH, 1957, AT 8 P.M.

Overture.

1. Comerford Troupe.

2. Dublin Globe Theatre Company.

3. Noel Purcell.

4. Leo McCabe.

5. Siobhan McKenna.

6. Rathmines and Rathgar Musical Society.

7. Gems from Italian Opera.
   Gabriella Tucci.
   Gianella Borelli.
   Antonio Galié.
   Giulio Mastrangelo.
   Accompanist : Robert Feist.

INTERVAL

8. Alice Dalgarno, Babs de Monte, and the Royalettes.
   Orchestra conducted by Jimmy Campbell.

9. Stanley Illsley.

10. Jack Cruice.

11. Josef Locke.

12. Micheal MacLiammoir.

13. O'D. Productions.
    Jimmy O'Dea.
    Maureen Potter.
    Vernon Hayden.

14. Finale.

COMPERE : HILTON EDWARDS.

Gaiety Theatre Augmented Orchestra conducted by Eamonn O Gallacobhair.

The Committee's thanks are due to the proprietors of the Gaiety Theatre (Dublin) Ltd., for putting the theatre at their disposal, free of charge; to the artists, members of the orchestra, and staff who have so generously given of their services free of charge, and to Messrs. McCullough who have kindly supplied the piano.

RAFFLE FOR PYE RADIO (SUPPLIED BY MESSRS. PIGOTTS). **TICKETS: 5 FOR 2/-**

SINNOTTS
THE WHISKEY HOUSE
OPPOSITE THE THEATRE

ABBEY BAR
★ On the North side

The Tom Daly Benefit Show in Dublin's Gaiety Theatre in April 1957, with Joe's prime spot towards the end of the show. (By kind permission of Brendan Hyland)

self-imposed purdah on Sunday 28 April 1957 to take part in a Benefit Gala at Dublin's Gaiety Theatre for the recently deceased Tom Daly, who had been stage-manager at the Gaiety for thirty years, and whom Joe had known from his early days there in 1941. The principal stars of Dublin's theatre world turned out on this occasion: Jimmy O'Dea, Vernon Hayden, Micheál MacLiammóir and Siobhán McKenna, with Hilton Edwards as compere. Joe, still a 'draw' with Dublin audiences despite being so long away, had one of the prime spots near the end of the show.

But by summer 1957, with Joseph at school in Dublin and Joe's activities increasingly centred there, Joe no longer had any need for a home in western Ireland. So he had put the Ballybunion house up for sale in May 1957. While it was on the market he sang at a Sunday show in Limerick's City Theatre in later June, and then with Mick Delahunty's 15-piece Dance Orchestra at the Super Ballroom, Listowel in July.

Joe was still in County Kerry in early August to crown Tralee's Carnival Queen at a dance in the CYMS Hall, the sort of thing a celebrity like Joe was now often asked to do.

Bertie Agnew

It was some time in 1957 that Joe met twenty-year old Roberta Agnew, having – it is said – first picked her out of the line-up of a beauty contest. Roberta, or Bertie as she was known, was from Northern Ireland, Belfast-born, and brought up in a family of eight children in Glengormley. She had moved to England in her late teens, initially to work as a secretary with the Midlands firm Coventry Glass. A good-looking girl with 'a figure to die for', she moved to London with the idea of becoming a model and was briefly engaged to an Englishman. When that relationship broke up, she left England for Dublin, hoping to make a fresh start. There she met Joe and fell under his spell. They soon became lovers. But Joe was not in a position to marry her, still having a wife in California; and Betty on her side was holding out from agreeing to divorce him as long as he held on to their son Joseph. Here was an impasse that was not easily resolved, and in the meantime Bertie was left in a kind of limbo.

On Report

In autumn 1957 Joe resumed touring with the Moss Empire theatre chain in England. He started off in the Winter Gardens in Morecambe, before moving to Oxford's New Theatre then to the Palace Theatre in Blackpool. After a short break he was in the London Hippodrome at the end of October, and then week after week in theatres mainly in the north of England until the end of December.

We get a revealing picture of what Joe was doing and how the tour went from a series of weekly report cards filled in by the different theatre managers *en route* and sent by them to the headquarters of the Moss chain in London. The report on Joe from Morecambe in September read: "Very good reception, this artist is still in good voice and is doing a much more straightforward act than on his previous visits, which is a great asset... His milking of the audience at the end of the act is still very much overdone and pointless, nevertheless he is working very well." At the Leeds Empire in November it was, "Exceptionally well received… in excellent voice and appearance, singing songs from comic opera together with the old Irish and sentimental numbers. [His performance was] undoubtedly a personal success." However, there was a caveat: "He seems to have lost his hold on the public which he had on his last visit." This last remark probably says as much about variety losing its appeal for 1957 audiences as it does about Joe. There was change in the air. The new stars in entertainment were young rock-and-roll singers like Tommy Steele.

Court Appearances

While Joe was performing at the Royalty Theatre in Chester in November 1957, he was summoned to the Manchester Assizes, to answer a claim for compensation lodged by the promoter Wyrill Heyworth relating to the concert tour he had organized for Joe seven years earlier. Heyworth alleged that Joe was guilty of a breach of contract, in that he hadn't sung at seven concerts set up for him in Wales and the West Country. Joe's defence was that he had had a throat ailment at the time and that he wasn't to blame. The judge ordered Joe to pay Heyworth £244. 7. 11d for the breach of contract, but allowed Joe's counter-claim for £240, leaving the impresario a derisory £4. 7. 11d. However Joe did have to pay seven-eighths of Heyworth's costs.

The second court case in which Joe was involved was a more embarrassing one. It was a paternity case brought by his 25-year-old former German housekeeper and nanny Margaret Pfeiffer. She had given birth to a daughter, Sigrid Rose, in a London hospital on 31 January 1957 and claimed that Joe was the father. She took out a case for child maintenance in the Dublin District Court, at which Joe was ordered to pay her £1 a week backdated to 1 February 1957. Joe wasn't present at the hearing, but through his counsel he denied that he was the father, a stance he maintained for the rest of his life.

Joe's third brush with the law came the following summer, on Monday 7 July 1958, in the High Court in Dublin when Joe – the litigant this time – claimed 700 guineas in unpaid fees for his 1956 summer appearances in Matthew Sullivan's ballroom in Ballybunion. Sullivan for his part denied that he had agreed to pay Joe a fixed fee for each appearance, and argued that the whole arrangement was an informal one between friends, with Joe staying at his hotel and being provided with meals, wines and cigars for about eight weeks free of charge. What's more, he had paid the airfare for Joe's son to fly from Shannon airport to New York.

Giving judgement, the President of the High Court said that there was a conflict in the testimonies of the two parties, but that he couldn't help noticing that their dealings with one another were conducted in 'anything but a strictly business atmosphere'. He therefore concluded on the balance of probabilities that there had been no strictly business arrangement between the two men that would have entitled Joe to the professional fees he was claiming. In the end the Judge found in favour of Sullivan and ordered Joe to pay both parties' legal fees.

King of the Panto

Joe's first theatre engagement of 1958 was as 'Guest Artist' in *Dick Whittington* at Dublin's Gaiety Theatre. Cecil Sheridan, the panto's director, was an old friend, as were others in the cast, a gather-up of his colleagues from the 1940s: Jimmy O'Dea and his wife Ursula Doyle, Maureen Potter and Micheál MacLiammóir. Joe was to play King Neptune and he appeared onstage only once, in Act 1, Scene 10 just after a 'spectacular under-water scene'. How King Neptune came to figure in a pantomime about Dick Whittington is anybody's guess, but pantomime is a generous medium.

Joe's contribution to the show was limited a few lines of dialogue, but followed by a medley of songs. And although his part seemed minimal in the script, it lasted onstage for at least twenty minutes – sometimes more – as Joe sang the songs for which he was

SCENE 10.

NEPTUNE: For in my long devoted reign (To C)
             There's none has challenged my domain,
             and where among survived Kings
             is one who sings (To D.S.)
             Like Neptune of the Seas (Back to Coach)
             They do just as I Please! (Sits)

CHORAL TAG: Mighty Neptune of the Seas.

                  (ENTER FAIRY R. OF NEPTUNE)

                     Music Cue 31.

FAIRY: Mighty Neptune, let me bring before you Dick
             Whittington - I need this lad to aid me in my
             fight against the cunning Rat.

NEPTUNE: Bring him before me.

                  (FAIRY moves U.C. for DICK'S ENTRANCE
                  DICK ENTERS. She brings him D.S.)

DICK: (KNEELING TO NEPTUNE) Grant me your protection,
             Mighty Ruler of the Seas. I will help the Fairy
             in her batter (MOVES R.)

NEPTUNE: (RISING) Bring my Royal Chariott and bid all
             creatures of the deep escort Dick Whittington
             to dry land. (TO C.)

                  Music Cue 32 - Fish comes on up C.
                  Electrics Cue 49.

                  Singing Finale.
                  House tabs down.
                  House tabs up for picture and down.

                  I N T E R V A L.

Joe's single page of dialogue as King Neptune in his own personal copy of the script of the 1958 pantomime, Dick Whittington. By this stage in his career, Joe was able to insist that his roles in panto were almost solely confined to singing.

best known and for which his audiences demanded encore after encore. These songs, of course, bore no relevance whatsoever to the plot of the panto, being nothing more than an opportunity for Joe to shine at what he did best.

There was, however, a minor hiccup at the start of the run. Joe appeared on the opening night but then missed the next two weeks – a chill caught in the under-water scene? – and Edward Mills, a bass, had to stand in for him. The panto, with Joe reinstated as 'King Neptune' then ran until 22 February 1958.

In March Joe made what was for him a rare excursion to the Republic's north-west counties, singing at the New Hall, Milford in County Donegal, and later in the month giving two sell-out concerts at the Gilhooly Hall in Sligo.

He was then back in Dublin in the second week of April 1958 to appear with English comedian Jimmy Edwards in *Whacko* at the Theatre Royal. Years later Edwards remembered his time in Dublin: "I was on the same bill as Josef Locke. Great fellow to give advice. Said we'd all be asked to these parties after the show. Said we should eat and drink as much as possible, but under no circumstances to give them a free cabaret. Minute the man was in the door he would start to sing and you couldn't stop him all night."

In May 1958 Joe was back in England. For the first time since 1953 he was signed up for a summer season in Blackpool, as guest artist in Ken Dodd's show *Let's Have Fun* on Central Pier. Then his wife Betty had been with him: now he was accompanied by Bertie and his six-year old son, Joseph. As Joe now longer owned a house in Blackpool, the three of them moved into rented accommodation for the summer. Bertie had just become pregnant with their first child, due in January the next year.

A Man of Property

Since he had returned to Ireland in 1955 Joe had been acquiring property in and around Dublin. He was an astute buyer, too, buying south of the Liffey where trade was reliable and brisk, and property rising in value. His first acquisitions were a row of three terrace houses on Nassau Street, which were rented out to businesses. In spring 1957 he bought the Moka Bar at 28 Anne Street South, just off Grafton Street, next door to The Crystal Ballroom, one of Dublin's busier nightspots. It was described as a 'flourishing, well-established, easily-run restaurant, espresso coffee and snack bar' and seated forty people. However, he didn't hold on to it for long, putting it up for sale again barely a year later on the grounds that he was shortly to return to Blackpool for the summer and would then be going on a tour of America and Canada.

The truth behind the sale, however, might be that he was increasingly coming under pressure from the tax authorities in England and needed the money.

THEATRE ROYAL
DUBLIN

HAROLD FIELDING Presents

WHACKO !

STARRING

JIMMY
EDWARDS

Guest Artist:
JOSEF
LOCKE

Commencing EASTER SUNDAY, 6th APRIL, 1958

Proprietors—Irish Cinemas Ltd.

Programme cover for Joe's week with comedian Jimmy Edwards at Dublin's Theatre Royal in April 1958. By this time, Joe was spending lengthy periods in Ireland.

The Taxman Cometh

In September 1957, when Joe was performing at the New Theatre in Oxford and suffering from the symptoms of Asian flu, he had been presented with a tax writ from the Inland Revenue. It was the first in a series of encounters with the tax authorities that were to earn Joe notoriety and culminate in what later became the best known episode in his life. The single thing that everyone would remember about Josef Locke: his flight from the taxman.

Early in 1958 Joe had been served with a tax bill for £10,411, based on his estimated earnings for the past three years. Joe had, of course, been out of the country for a good part of that time and, as we know, had not been performing or earning on a regular basis. In any case, he said he had been assured by his manager Lew Grade that all his back taxes had been paid. So Joe simply ignored the demand and carried on regardless. Faced with neither payment nor response from Joe, the Inland Revenue waited a few months before filing a claim for non-payment in early autumn 1958. The choice was clear: either he paid up or he would be made bankrupt and all his assets in the United Kingdom seized.

But Joe continued to stick his head in the sand, and so the bankruptcy process was started in Blackpool. A first meeting of Joe's creditors was held at the end of September, and a week later, on 7 October 1958, Joe himself met with James Tye, the Official Receiver. Just three days before this meeting, on 4 October, the Irish press reported that the Moka Bar had been sold to Mr. Albert Smets, who reopened it as an exclusive café-restaurant called 'New Amsterdam'. So Joe had managed to free up some cash to meet his liabilities, even if not enough and, significantly, not within the jurisdiction of the English court.

Joe's high profile in Blackpool ensured that the local press provided regular updates on his tax troubles throughout the autumn. Joe undoubtedly fed the journalists many of these stories, as he was invariably quoted verbatim. For example, Joe said he had been advised by his accountant that the claim for back-tax was 'ridiculous'; and that there was no justification for him being made bankrupt. As 'evidence' for this he was quoted as saying that he had one son (Joseph) at 'a good school' and 'another about to go there', and any stigma of bankruptcy would affect them.[2] On and on it went, almost on a weekly basis: the press, if not actually taking Joe's side, at least putting the case for the defence, while the Official Receiver and Inland Revenue, as one might expect, said nothing.

On 23 September Joe flatly denied, in the face of rumours to the contrary, that he had any intention of absconding to Ireland. He had only just then returned from Dublin where he had been visiting his parents and was definitely not planning to do a 'flit'. "I'm staying here. There's no reason for me to leave the country – I have nothing at all to be ashamed of." A few days later he announced that he was going to meet with the Receiver, and "I will have a bombshell to drop… I have been taxed for money I

[2] *This was a distinctly odd thing for him to say as he had only one son, Joseph, that we know anything about at this time.*

haven't earned." And so this cat-and-mouse game continued for days going into weeks – Joe planting stories in the local press and the Official Receiver's Office in Manchester declining to comment.

For the rest of October the Receiver repeatedly sent Joe reminders to meet with him, but he didn't appear. A final reminder was sent by registered post to Walsh's Ballroom in Listowel, County Kerry: the contact address Joe had given to the Court. But by early November there had been no response to that letter either. Possibly Joe never received the letter, since on Sunday 9 November he was in Dublin – not in Listowel – appearing in a prestigious Variety Club of Ireland show in the Theatre Royal. This was their annual show and there was always fierce competition between the great and the good of the Irish entertainment world to appear in it. In 1958 it was called *Shake Hands with the Irish,* echoing the name of the film (*Shake Hands with the Devil*) which American actor James Cagney was then filming in Dublin. Cagney too was to be star of the show, and Joe may not have wanted to be left out.

Nevertheless Joe was back in Blackpool the following evening, on Monday 10 November, for the tail-end of the season and to resume his skirmishes with the Receiver. But something – we don't what – happened to change his mind, and within the week he was to renege on his previous declarations that he wouldn't abscond, and had fled back to Ireland.

The Flight into Ireland

Joe's account of his flight from the taxman gained much in the re-telling over the years. According to the version he gave to Gay Byrne's 1984 *Late Late Show*, "I took the Rolls and the Jaguar and any good-looking blonde I could lay my hands on and went back to Dublin." That gave a touch of swagger to what might otherwise have seemed a less than glorious scuttling for cover.

And in truth, far from it being a defiant cocking a snook at the Inland Revenue that Joe sometimes made it out to be, his departure from England was understandably a low-profile affair. Fred Holloway, a worker at one of the Blackpool garages, was asked to collect Joe and 'a woman and a small child' (Bertie and Joseph) from his employer's house in St. Annes on a dark November evening and drive them to the Liverpool Docks. The garage's Morris van was loaded up with suitcases and a large wicker basket, and they set out. However, as they got to the outskirts of the Docks, Joe asked for them to be dropped off, saying that they would take a taxi the rest of the way. He thanked the driver and gave him a five-pound note for his trouble. That night they caught the ferry to Dublin.

The Bankruptcy Court met on Wednesday 19 November. In view of the fact that Joe had failed to attend several meetings with the Receiver and had also failed to reply to the registered letter addressed to him in Listowel, the presiding Registrar W.J. Plant said he had no option but to issue a warrant for the arrest of Joseph McLaughlin, "on the grounds that there is no evidence to show that the bankrupt has a reasonable excuse for not being present today."

No appearance at bankruptcy court

REGISTRAR ISSUES A WARRANT FOR ARREST OF JOSEF LOCKE

A WARRANT for the arrest of Josef Locke, the Irish tenor, was issued by the Registrar, Mr W. J. Plant, at Blackpool Bankruptcy Court today where he failed to appear for his public examination in bankruptcy in his own name of Joseph McLaughlin.

"This bankrupt has absconded and is now in Southern Ireland." said Mr J. Tye, the Official Receiver.

The headline in Blackpool's Evening Gazette on the day of the arrest warrant. (Evening Gazette, 19 November 1958)

But Joe was already gone, beyond the reach of the Inland Revenue and the Bankruptcy Court. He was also, inevitably, turning his back on a fourteen-year-long singing career in England, which had seen him mature from a struggling opera singer to being the biggest-selling recording star in Britain.

The day after the Bankruptcy Court hearing Joe was photographed at the Ballsbridge Bloodstock Sales in Dublin. He had paid a sum, reputed to be 790 guineas, for two horses to take back to his farm in County Meath. With his usual sense of mischief he called one of them 'The Taxman'.

CHAPTER SEVEN

The Happy Exile?
1958-1967

A Fresh Start

Whatever the reality of Joe's flight from Blackpool in November 1958, he didn't return to Dublin a broken man, nor did he, as some have said, 'lie low in Ireland for a few years'. Far from it. He immediately plunged into property dealing, including a hotel and a pub, buying racehorses, and giving the occasional concert. He took up again with Jimmy O'Dea and many of his old friends in variety, and was to join them in an overseas tour. Indeed he did much more travelling during the 1960s, making several transatlantic trips and circling the globe in a way he had not done before. And Joe made new connections too: literary figures like Brendan Behan, with whom he shared a taste for Guinness and living on the edge. And, not least, in Irish horse-racing circles.

Within a few weeks of being back in Ireland Joe was performing in the Arundel Ballroom in Waterford, accompanied by Alan Lawless and his Radio Nirvana Eight-Piece Orchestra. However he had made no provision for resuming his career in Ireland and it was not until spring 1959 that he signed up with the Irish Theatrical Agency to organize and handle his bookings. In the meantime he did one or two gigs a month.

Joe and Bertie were at this time living together in Dublin. Bertie was known as 'Mrs. Locke' to the neighbours, who had no suspicion of there being another Mrs. Locke alive and well, and living in California. With Joe and Bertie's first baby – Joe's sixth daughter and his seventh child – born in January 1959, they were keen to get married. So Joe flew out to California in the summer, with the object of persuading Betty to agree to a divorce.

Betty was then trying to establish a modelling career in Los Angeles, where her mother and brother were also living, and was settled in her new life. Their son Joseph was still living in Dublin with Joe. Increasingly he was to be wrangled over in the marital struggle between his parents.

California Dreamin'

If a 'softly, softly' approach was what Joe had in mind in visiting Betty that summer, it didn't last long. The actor Roger Moore was their neighbour in an apartment opposite. Moore and his wife Dorothy Squires had known Joe many years earlier on the English

variety circuit, and he took to dropping in on them in the evenings 'to chew the fat' and, as it turned out, to provide them with almost daily updates on the parlous state of his marriage. His wife was a 'lazy tart' who had never made his breakfast for him. She was fixated on her mother. She objected to his bad language – "which is fecking terrible for me" – and was driving him mad.

What followed, according to Moore, hardly showed Joe in a good light. He tricked Betty into signing a document to transfer into his own account money he had previously deposited in her name in a Dublin bank. Then, while she was out, he collected all the furs he had given her over the years in two suitcases and brought them over to Moore and Squires' apartment for safe-keeping. Finally, after she had left him and gone to stay with her mother, Joe raided the mother's apartment and made off with Betty's jewellery. He could, Moore noted, 'be a real bastard'.

He could be a charmer as well. Moore admired the way he could handle an audience, inviting people to call out their song requests and then, in the ensuing hubbub, asking suavely "Did you say 'I'll take you home again, Kathleen'?" or whatever song he was going to sing in the first place. On another occasion when out driving he was stopped for some traffic infringement by a local cop, who just happened to be Irish, and Joe turned on the Irish accent and 'blarneyed' so effectively that he got off scot-free.

However in the autumn, when he returned to Ireland, he was no nearer getting Betty to agree to a divorce than before. By then Bertie's first child, Nikki, was eight months old.

Dublin Fisticuffs

In March of the following year Joe found himself in a Dublin district court charged with assault. It involved Jack Brewster, a man in his fifties, whose wife Biddy ran a Marriage Bureau in Dublin city centre, in one of three terrace properties which Joe owned along Nassau Street, opposite the southside of Trinity College.[1]

It seems that Joe had been passing along Nassau Street on his way to the Olympia Theatre when he came across Brewster standing at the open door of the house smoking his pipe. As landlord Joe had asked for the door of the Marriage Bureau always to be kept closed, and he reminded Brewster of this. In the heated argument that followed Joe was said to have used 'very offensive language'. There was a scuffle. In attempting to snatch Brewster's pipe from his mouth, Joe broke Brewster's tooth and cut his lip, at which point Mrs. Brewster, fearing, she said, for her husband's life, called the Guards. The District Judge took a poor view of Joe's behaviour, especially given Brewster's age, and fined him £20.

Joe had a history of mixing it with people. Ray Galton, the scriptwriter with Alan Simpson of a 1950s radio show *Star Bill*, recalled an incident when Terry-Thomas, the show's star, complained about a sketch they had written for him, and kept on and on about it right through the rehearsal, until Joe, who was the guest singer that week, lost patience, picked him up by the scruff of the neck and said, "If you don't shut up and do these lads' script, I'll knock you right through this fucking door." It had the desired effect. The comedian Jimmy Jewel said that on another occasion he had held a knife theatrically to Joe's throat and threatened to cut his head off if he didn't stop belting members of a Blackpool summer show. It was a reputation Irish compere Hal Roach seized upon when he spotted Joe coming in late to one of his shows. "Come on in, Joe," he said from the stage, "Make yourself at home – hit somebody." Joe, it was said, loved it and 'lapped up the laughs'.

First time at the Olympia

Joe had begun performing at Dublin's Olympia Theatre in the week of the assault, his first one-week run in Ireland since leaving Blackpool. His support acts were a 'cross-channel' group of variety artists, including Barry Young, a Scots singer and step-dancer, and an orchestra conducted by Bram Rooney. Joe was accompanied on piano by Marie Whelan.

Apart from this short run in Dublin and another one-off concert in Cork City Hall on Sunday 3 April, Joe doesn't seem to have done much performing in 1960. Family matters may have taken up much of his time. Bertie had their second child Karl that

---

[1] *Biddy Brewster's advertisements in the Irish Times for her Dublin Marriage Society offered 'opportunities for Protestant professional and business men' to meet prospective – and suitable – Protestant partners, and for 'Church of Ireland ladies, county background, to meet gentlemen with farming or professional interests'. She claimed to cater for 'non-Protestants' as well, but stressed that there were 'separate R.C. and Protestant departments' and 'religious safeguards'.*

year, Joe's eighth child, and his second son. But even in these early days – the couple were barely three years together – Joe and Bertie's relationship was showing signs of strain, not helped by the fact that Betty still refused to give Joe a divorce.

The Property Magnate

The other factor pushing his singing into second place was that during the early 1960s Joe was expanding his property portfolio. As already mentioned, he had acquired the three terrace houses in Nassau Street. To these he now added two more sizeable properties. The first of these, in February 1961, was the historic Corn Exchange Building on Dublin's Burgh Quay, where Daniel O'Connell had once held his Repeal meetings. His partner in the purchase was a Mr. Stephenson, the owner of an auction and valuation business in Grafton Street. Together they paid around £40,000,[2] and formed 'The Corn Exchange Building Company Ltd' to manage and oversee the running of the building. It may have been an expensive buy, but it was also a lucrative investment, bringing in an annual rent of around £8,000, the equivalent of almost £130,000 today.

The second major property acquisition was the Listowel Arms Hotel in County Kerry in March 1961, for which he paid around £20,000. The thirty-five bedroom hotel had a beautiful setting, in the town's main square but with a view from the back of the premises over the famous race-course. Joe renamed the hotel The White Horse Inn, a reference to the musical from which his customary closing number 'Goodbye' was taken. But it was probably, too, a sideways wink – or perhaps, in Joe's case, a respectful doffing of his cap – to the local horse-racing fraternity.

During his first year of ownership Joe began building a ballroom extension, and while the work was ongoing, took over personal supervision of the hotel, spending the summer there and getting to know the ropes of the hospitality business. When the liquor licence was transferred to Joe's name at the Listowel Civil Bill Court in April 1961, the magistrate joked, in response to Joe confirming – as the law required – that he was conversant with the licensing laws, "You possibly had the advantage of learning them from all angles."

The hotel and new ballroom were officially opened in the last week of September 1961, to coincide with the town being thronged with crowds for the annual Listowel races. As refurbished, the hotel had twenty-four bedrooms, many ensuite. Joe proudly declared that he could have filled ten times that number of rooms during Race Week. He was also proud of his new ballroom with its Canadian maple floor which could accommodate one thousand dancers at a time or four hundred people sitting. He had ambitious plans eventually to extend the ballroom 'right over the River Feale', so that it could hold two and a half thousand people.

On that opening night of Sunday 24 September Joe himself was the star attraction, with Jack Barrett's 'Orchestra' – in fact, a Ceili Band – as support act. He went on to sing in the ballroom every night that week, and often in the Cocktail Bar – shyly called

---

[2] *Joe's financial dealings in Dublin were in Irish pounds, then called 'punts', which were roughly equivalent in value to English pounds.*

Joe's Bar – where he charmed drinkers with his relaxed easy manner and impromptu performances. Within earshot of the press, he laughed off suggestions that his voice had gone, a story put about, he said, by critics when he had left England three years before.

'Ireland Sings' Down Under

Joe used the occasion of the hotel's opening to announce that he was shortly to leave for a tour of Australia and New Zealand. A few weeks later Joe joined an assorted troupe of Irish performers to embark on a month-long trip to the Southern Hemisphere. The party met up in New York, Joe having gone on ahead to take young Joseph to California to stay with his mother. According to Bertie, Joe was to take this opportunity to ask Betty – yet again – for a divorce.

The party included pianist Charles Lynch, soprano Minnie Clancy and Joe's old boss Jimmy O'Dea. Joe and O'Dea got top billing on the tour, being the two most likely to pull in the crowds. Jack Barrett and his Ceili Band provided the Irish jigs and

An advert in the New Zealand press in 1961 for the Night in Eire show presented by Joe and his party of fellow Irish performers (New Zealand Herald, 17 October 1961)

reels that expatriate Irish audiences expected. Before the tour party left, there was detailed planning and discussion about terms, payments and fees. Veteran actor Vernon Hayden was compere throughout and acted as 'guardian angel' to the entertainers, with responsibility for their well-being and good behaviour.

Their two shows, *Ireland Sings* and *A Night in Eire*, were unashamedly targeted at the Irish Diaspora 'down under'. They featured predominantly Irish traditional music plus an assortment of excerpts from the classical repertoire. The classical pieces were intended to show off the artists' musical versatility, while the Irish elements purveyed a romanticized view of the Ireland many emigrants had left behind. Binding the whole thing together with humour was O'Dea and his comic creation 'Biddy Mulligan, the pride of the Coombe'.

The tour started in New Zealand, with a concert in Wellington Town Hall on Saturday 14 October 1961, followed by performances on successive evenings the following week in Auckland, Palmerston, Christchurch, and back to Wellington. At each venue audiences gave the cast an enthusiastic reception, the Maoris in particular taking the Irish entertainers to their hearts. Reviews said that they were 'insatiable in their demands for encores'.

Joe with his old friend (and first boss), Jimmy O'Dea enjoying a drink in Neary's Bar, Chatham Street, Dublin in April 1958. The stage door to the Gaiety Theatre was directly opposite the rear entrance to Neary's, making it a popular haunt for actors, singers and entertainers. (Irish Photographic Archive).

The party left New Zealand for Australia on Sunday 22 October, to begin a further exhausting two weeks' touring coast to coast. There were concerts in Sydney, Melbourne, Canberra, Adelaide and Perth. In the main, the Australian press was complimentary to the Irish tourists, one reviewer commenting, "Sydney Stadium leapt into lilting life and rhythm last night… nor were [the artists'] talents confined to Irish Airs and Jigs." Joe, advertised as 'The biggest personality on the Irish stage', was a 'beguiling Irish tenor', whose rendering of 'Take a Pair of Sparkling Eyes' "would have made one believe Sir Arthur Sullivan was born in Dublin." (Didn't he know that Sullivan's father – the surname is a giveaway – was born in Ireland?) Not all the reviews were favourable: one critic likened the show to 'a Parish Hall in Ballyhooley'.

When the tour was over, O'Dea and the others travelled back to Ireland via Canada, where they had a booking in Toronto, while Joe flew to California, ostensibly to make some recordings in Los Angeles, but mainly to collect young Joseph and take him back to Ireland. Having returned home with his son to Dublin in the second half of November, Joe went straight into rehearsal for the upcoming Gaiety Christmas pantomime *Mother Goose*, in which he was to star alongside Milo O'Shea and Maureen Potter. By now, the Locke couple were expecting their third child, Peter (in March 1962), so the family moved into a larger house, 28 St. Thomas Mead in Dublin's Mount Merrion area. So, what with rehearsals, moving house and looking after his growing property and business interests, Joe had little time left for shows or concerts for several months after the Gaiety pantomime ended in the New Year.

Last Night of the Theatre Royal

During this period Joe was dividing his time between Dublin and Ballybunion, where he had rented a house convenient to Listowel and from where he could keep an eye on what was happening in his hotel. But on Saturday 30 June 1962 an event took place in Dublin that urgently recalled him to the capital: the final closing performance in Dublin's Theatre Royal.

The Theatre Royal on Hawkins Street was a huge building, housing a theatre, cinema, winter-garden and restaurant. In its day it had been the biggest theatre in Europe, able to hold four thousand people and with a large, roomy stage. It had been Dublin's most popular venue for variety, concerts, pantomimes and comedies, circuses, and even boxing matches. Many celebrated artists, like Bob Hope, James Cagney and Judy Garland, had played there. Dubliners knew it simply as 'The Royal', loving it for its old-world elegance and air of luxury. Joe too, as 'Joseph McLaughlin' had sung operatic duets there with May Devitt some twenty years before, at the very outset of his career. Sadly, however, in its final days the audiences were not big enough and it had lost money. Its fate was to be demolished to make way for a new cinema and multi-storey office block.

On its final night Joe joined other 'old favourites of the house', Jimmy O'Dea, Noel Purcell, Jack Cruise and Cecil Sheridan, onstage to bring down the curtain for the last time on one hundred and forty-one years of show-business and entertainment. In his valedictory speech the comedian Cecil Sheridan described 'The Royal' as a place with "a big heart, big capacity and big audiences."For those present it was a 'night of throat-catching and heart-tugging experiences'. Each of the invited artists gave their all.

But it was 'Big Joe', critics said, who best captured the mood of the evening, encouraging his fellow artists to 'Blaze Away' regardless, and bidding everyone a last 'Goodbye'. The *Irish Press* correspondent reported that 'the great house was in an enthusiastic uproar' at his performance. But perhaps Joe overdid the nostalgia on this occasion. There's a story that as he walked offstage after his last song he remarked to Cecil Sheridan, 'You know, that song haunts me'. "So it should," the answer shot back, "You're after feckin' murderin' it!"

The following week there was an auction of the theatre's fixtures, fittings and 'front of house effects'. Joe was there over the three days, buying two hundred and twenty seats from the auditorium at twenty-seven shillings each, and a further one hundred from another buyer who had bought more than he needed. Quizzed by curious press reporters about what he was going to do with them, he gave two different stories: the first that he planned to open a small cinema in Dublin; the second that it was to be a small 'legitimate' theatre.

With the exception of the closing night of 'The Royal' Joe seemed to have stopped giving solo concerts, shows or singing appearance. Irish audiences might have been forgiven for thinking that he had retired from performing or disappeared abroad on tour again. But he was to re-surface in a new medium, television, in July 1962 when he gave the first of what were to be a number of appearances in coming decades, as a guest singer on Gay Byrne's *Late Late Show*.

Variety at the Gaiety

The closure of the Theatre Royal might have seemed to signal the disappearance of variety from Dublin stages, as had happened with variety in England. But the, by now, veteran theatre impresario Louis Elliman chose to swim against the tide and announced an experimental series of shows at the Gaiety Theatre for autumn 1962. It was to be called *Gaiety at Eight*, with just one performance per night, probably modelled on Glasgow's successful *Five Past Eight Show*. Needing someone guaranteed to pull in the crowds, Elliman engaged Joe to 'top the bill' for three weeks.

Joe entered enthusiastically into rehearsals for the new show, but the weekend before the first night, when contracts had been signed and the show was ready to roll, he received an unexpected invitation from the United States to do an American tour, to start immediately. He was to have a solo concert at the Lincoln Centre in New York for three thousand dollars, followed by gigs in Chicago, Detroit, San Francisco and Toronto. The last four were to be on a percentage basis – which of course, would have been greatly to Joe's advantage. He stood to make a lot of money out of it.

Even for a performer as celebrated as Joe, this was a dazzling prospect. Unfortunately,

THEATRE ROYAL, DUBLIN

SATURDAY, 30th JUNE, 1962, at 8 p.m.

"ROYALE FINALE"

1. "PROLOGUE" ... ... Jimmy Campbell and the Theatre Royal Orchestra.
2. "SHOW BUSINESS" ... ... Frankie Blowers, Peggy Dell, Royalettes, Jimmy Campbell Singers.
3. "TREBLE TROUBLE" ... Cecil Sheridan, Mickser Reid, John Molloy, Derry O'Donovan.
4. "MUSICAL COCKTAIL" ... Jimmy Campbell Singers.
5. "A ROYAL OCCASION" ... Cecil Sheridan and John Molloy.
6. ENSEMBLE ... ... Alice Dalgarno, Babs de Monte, Royalettes, Cora Cadwell Dancers and the Jimmy Campbell Singers.

INTERVAL:

"ROYAL CABARET"

OUR GUESTS :

Frankie Blowers	Edmund Browne	Jack Cruise
Paddy Crosbie	Danny Cummins	Ursula Doyle
Val Fitzpatrick	Pauline Forbes	Vernon Hayden
Frank Howard	Josef Locke	Sean Mooney
Jimmy O'Dea	Harry O'Donovan	Noel Purcell
Milo O'Shea		

Mickser Reid   Cecil Sheridan

Choreography and Design : Alice Dalgarno and Babs De Monte

The Jimmy Campbell Singers :

Kay Condron   Denis Claxton   Claire Kelleher   Bill Golding   Dolores Murphy

The Royalettes

JIMMY CAMPBELL and the THEATRE ROYAL ORCHESTRA

TOMMY DANDO

The running order for the last night at Dublin's Theatre Royal on Saturday 30 June 1962. (Author's own collection)

committed as he already was to Elliman and his Gaiety show, it was not one he was able to follow up. Who knows, then, with what mixed feelings he took to the Gaiety stage on 18 October 1962 alongside Irish comedian Danny Cummins, Johnny Victory, Brenda Doyle and the Royalettes? As so often with Joe and America, it was a case of what might have been.

Domestic Troubles

It was during this Gaiety run that Joe was involved in a fracas with Bertie that cast a harsh light on their domestic difficulties. What exactly happened in the family kitchen in the afternoon of 1 November 1962 was later hotly disputed. Joe claimed that Bertie had emptied a pot of stew over him and hit him over the head with a saucepan; and that he had simply acted in self-defence. Bertie for her part said that she had been the victim of an unprovoked attack in the course of which Joe had fallen on top of her breaking her leg.

Whatever the rights and wrongs of the matter, a child was then sent to get help from the neighbours. Two neighbours then tried to make Bertie comfortable and called for a doctor, who gave her an injection and had her taken by ambulance to Baggot Street Hospital. There, she was diagnosed with a fracture in her right leg, consistent, the medical report said, "with either a severe fall or with some weight falling on her leg," The leg was set in plaster and she was treated for 'pain and shock'. She also had some bruising too, described as 'black marks', on her neck and arms.

Three days later Garda officers visited Joe at home, told him that Bertie had lodged a formal complaint against him, and issued him with a caution. Joe agreed to present himself at Kevin Street Garda Station later that day, where he was cautioned a second time. After treatment in hospital Bertie was able to walk with the aid of crutches, and she returned to the family home to spend Christmas with Joe and the children. The couple then left for Spain in the New Year, initially for a short holiday.

In the midst of this family bust-up, Joe had continued his business dealings. In a surprise move at the end of December 1962, he sold The White Horse Inn, which he had owned for just under two years, to a consortium of local businessmen, 'Listowel Arms Ltd', who immediately changed it back to its original name. Either Joe had tired of the hotel business or needed once again to free up some cash.

All's Well That Ends Well?

If Joe hoped that Bertie and he would be able to resolve matters between them in Spain, he was disappointed. She refused to drop the charges she had brought against him, the chief one being that of 'wilful and malicious wounding'. The first court hearing was in Dublin in mid-February 1963, but the case was adjourned for six months because Bertie, the principal witness, was abroad and unable to testify. In the meantime Joe, who had returned from Spain for the hearing, was remanded on his own bail.

Bertie Agnew, described as 'Mrs Bertie Locke' at the Leopardstown Races in June 1962, accompanied by Mrs. Nora Girvan.

Shortly after the hearing Joe took Joseph, and Bertie's three children back with him to Spain to meet up with their mother. Foreseeing a longer stay, he rented a villa and chartered a yacht for the family to go sailing. But the presence of the children didn't have the mollifying effect Joe might have hoped. In what was almost a repeat of the previous incident Bertie fired a pot of boiling water in Joe's direction that had three lobsters cooking inside. As for the yacht, during another spat Bertie threw the diamond engagement ring Joe had bought for her over the side into the sea.

In April 1963, in a fresh development, Joe paid for Bertie to fly to Canada to stay with her sister. She was still there in early August at the time of the second hearing, which led to the case being adjourned for a second time. At the third and final hearing on 30 August, with Bertie still in Canada and seemingly meaning to stay there, the prosecution case against Joe failed, on the narrow legal grounds that 'wounding' required that the skin be 'visibly broken' and medical evidence showed that this wasn't so with Bertie.

Cleared of the wounding charge, Joe emerged jubilant from court. As he stood on the court steps, he confounded the waiting press with the statement: "Now that the case is over, Bertie is coming back. We are going to get married in Dublin. We realize that it was only a domestic quarrel." Their wedding, Joe went on, would take place 'as soon as possible.' He omitted to mention the central impediment to the marriage – that there was a current 'Mrs. Locke' to whom he was still married.

However Bertie did not return from Canada 'as soon as possible,' and in September 1963 she had even taken a job there working as a receptionist. As for the three younger children left in his care, Joe must have been at his wits' end. He tried sending them to Derry where his brother's wife looked after them for a while. At another time he put them on a plane to Bertie in Canada where they lived for a few months, hoping that this would bring her back. But these were temporary solutions that didn't address the main problem.

The Ha'Penny Inn

With the court case behind him and flush with the money from the sale of his Listowel hotel Joe could turn his attention once more to acquiring property in Dublin city centre.[3] In September 1963 he bought Murray's Bar on Wellington Quay, a popular three-storey Victorian pub on the banks of the Liffey. He renamed it The Ha'penny Inn, as it was adjacent to the quaint Ha'penny Bridge over the river. The pub was well-positioned for passing trade. It had a ground floor bar and a second bar on the first floor, with living accommodation on the floor above. Joe moved into this upstairs flat, in effect 'living above the shop'.

He kept the press informed of his plans for the pub, saying that he intended to renovate it completely and develop it as a cabaret club with nightly shows. He voiced the hope that this "would do something towards relieving unemployment among variety artists in the city." Perhaps he felt it would lend fresh impetus to his own career which seemed to be in the doldrums. Might he not also, after months resting up in Spain, have welcomed the buzz that running a pub in Dublin's city centre would give him?

The official re-opening of the bar as The Ha'penny Inn took place on 10 December 1963. For Dublin this was a celebrity occasion, with Jimmy O'Dea and his wife Ursula Doyle as the principal guests. The renovated pub had a 'singing lounge', a new manager and twelve bar staff. There was an initial setback some three weeks later when seven hundred and sixty pounds was stolen from the pub safe and till in what was described as 'a daring daylight robbery': the padlocked door of the pub being forced open on a Sunday afternoon while the manager and the staff were gone to lunch. Undeterred Joe pressed ahead and installed a piano in the upstairs bar, ready for the start of the cabaret shows. It had to be brought in via an upstairs window, causing something of a stir on Wellington Quay.

Dubliner Maurice Colgan recalls that as a young man in his twenties, home on holidays from England, he was walking along the quays when he heard someone singing in the Ha'Penny Inn, then familiarly known in Dublin as 'Joe's Place'. Out of curiosity Colgan went inside and upstairs to the first floor lounge where he saw Joe standing on a low stage singing one of his ballads. Joe's voice and stage-presence made an immediate impression on him. As the evening wore on, the audience kept on at Joe to sing something more, and it was very late – even early morning – before he finished singing. Colgan wanted to get the singer's autograph for his mother, but had nothing for him to write on except the inside of an empty packet of Capstan Full Strength. Joe, laughing, signed his name nevertheless. Then, called upon for a final encore, he strode back to the stage and launched into 'Goodbye', his usual closing number.

But for all Joe's grand plans for it, the pub's proximity to the river and the docks meant that it attracted among its clientele a high proportion of dockers and seamen, not to mention the prostitutes and other detrimentals that hung about them. It acquired, or perhaps couldn't shake off, a sleazy reputation as a 'rough' joint.

---

[3] *At this time Joe seems to have been involved in several speculative purchases in Dublin city centre, not all of which have come to light.*

BY INSTRUCTION OF THE DIRECTORS

THE OLYMPIA THEATRE

DAME STREET, DUBLIN 2

FOR SALE BY AUCTION

(UNLESS PREVIOUSLY SOLD PRIVATELY)

On Thursday, 10th October, 1963

AT 3 P.M.

AT

THE SHELBOURNE HOTEL, DUBLIN

AUCTIONEERS:

JACKSON-STOPS & McCABE,

ESTATE HOUSE, 62, DAWSON STREET, DUBLIN 2.

Telephone: 71177 (5 Lines)

and at

LONDON, NORTHAMPTON, CHESTER, YORK, CHICHESTER, YEOVIL,
CIRENCESTER & NEWMARKET.

SOLICITORS:

MESSRS. T. P. ROBINSON & CO.,

ULSTER BANK CHAMBERS,
3 LOWER O'CONNELL STREET, DUBLIN 1.

J. T. Drought, Ltd., Printers, Dublin.

'The one that got away': the 1963 auction sheet for Dublin's Olympia Theatre. (Author's own collection)

The façade of Dublin's Olympia Theatre in 1960, when Joe first performed there. It was to become one of his favourite theatres in Ireland to which he often returned perform, particularly in the later 1970s and 1980s.

The One That Got Away

By the middle of 1964 Joe's singing career in Ireland had still not taken off to any significant extent. He had done a few recorded radio shows for Radio Éireann, such as guesting in Noel Purcell's *Christmas Hamper Show* on Christmas Day 1963, but no live concerts anywhere in the country. He was reduced, it must sometimes have seemed, to singing on his own turf in The Ha'penny Inn. There was nothing to compare with his frenetic activity of a decade earlier, when he was singing twice nightly in theatres the length and breadth of England, Scotland and Wales.

His personal life was no better. Bertie had returned to Ireland for three weeks in summer 1964 to see her children, but then went back to Canada again. Joe had had to send her money for clothes and for the fare home, as she had previously cashed in the return half of the plane ticket he had bought for her in Spain because she was short of money.

It was in August 1964, when Joe's professional and personal fortunes were at a low ebb, that an opportunity presented itself to acquire a property close to his heart. It was Dublin's Olympia Theatre in Dame Street, where he had performed a couple of times since his return to Ireland. Its owners had found it increasingly difficult to make it pay, and many other theatres in Ireland and England, like Joe's old stomping-ground the Belfast Empire, were having to close. But Joe was confident he could turn things around and make the Olympia profitable. "I will run the theatre as a theatre, with straight plays and variety and cabaret on the style of the London Hippodrome."

Joe had previously offered £80,000 for the Olympia in July 1963. It had been turned down by the owners at the time, and then disposed of at public auction for exactly that amount in October while he was abroad. This time Joe was determined not to let the theatre slip out of his grasp. He offered £100,000 to its new London-based owners, who were planning its conversion to a ballroom. During negotiations in Dublin's Gresham Hotel, he raised his offer by £5000, but refused to go higher when the vendors hinted that another £15,000 might clinch the deal. It could be that the London Group, led by Monaghan-born Tommy Gorman, were just stringing him along. Whatever the reason, Joe's bid was not accepted, and he failed to acquire one of Dublin's oldest theatres, which would have been the 'jewel in the crown' of his property empire.

In the event the theatre was saved from being turned into a ballroom by a local consortium led by theatre producer Brendan Smith, who leased it from the London Group while the latter's planning applications for demolition and conversion were turned down over and over again by Dublin Corporation. In this way the theatre was kept open and in local hands. But Joe bore no grudge at the failure of his bids. He retained his fondness for the old 1879 'Grande Dame' theatre, returning to perform there a number of times in the next two decades.

The Hand-Over, Shut-Down and Takeaway

Autumn 1965 brought no easing of Joe's family problems. His son Joseph, by now thirteen, ran away from their home in Greystones, County Wicklow on 9 September and was listed as 'missing' by the Gardaí. He had gone off once before, in 1960, on his way home from school only to be found twenty-four hours later gazing into a shop window in Rathmines. This latest escapade was altogether more serious. He hitch-hiked north to Belfast and turned up on the doorstep of some family friends. Aware of how things were between Joe and Betty, and unsure how to proceed, these friends contacted a children's charity (NSPCC). Joseph was then placed in a temporary foster home, while both parents were contacted. His mother Betty flew in immediately from California and was reunited with Joseph at a friend's house. It had been four years since she had last seen him, in autumn 1961 when Joe was touring Australia.

Joe finally had to admit defeat. Being unable to go to Belfast to fetch Joe back– as his outstanding arrest warrant applied in Northern Ireland too – he signed a document giving Betty sole custody of the boy and permitting her to take him back permanently to live with her in California. He explained in a letter to her that he did so in Joseph's best interests. Mother and son left for America in October 1965. In the years that followed Joseph and his father saw little of one another, and Joseph largely lost contact with his half-brothers and sisters.

While all this was going on, Joe had trouble of a different kind, over the sacking of an employee at The Ha'penny Inn. The Irish National Union of Vintners, Grocers and Allied Trades Assistants took up the case and began an action for 'unfair dismissal', picketing the premises and calling the remaining bar-staff out on strike. Joe's response – as ever, impetuous and headstrong – was to clear all the stock from the pub, lock up the premises, and to serve notice on the entire staff.

To compound his miseries, there was a burglary at his house in Greystones. The Gardaí listed some of the stolen items in the Dublin newspapers. It made for impressive reading: "a large gold platinum and diamond ring with three cross-over snakes, a silver blue mink stole, worth £460; and a solid gold Rolex Oyster wrist watch, valued at £275." Clearly Joe had not lost his taste for expensive, luxury goods. And was he still holding on to one of Betty's furs?

In a further development, in autumn 1965 Bertie finally returned from Canada to Ireland. She was to claim later that this was a last attempt at reconciliation with Joe. She rented accommodation for herself and the children near his house in Greystones, and Joe took to dropping around and taking them out for meals.

On Christmas Day 1965 Joe gave what had become for him a rare public performance, on *The Christmas Hamper Show* on Radio Éireann, singing 'some of the biggest hits from his stage and recording performances', accompanied by 'The Town Hall Chorus'. If 1965 had been his *annus horribilis*, this seemed like a glimmer of light at the darkest time of year.

The Final Break-Up

But it was a false dawn. If Joe had any hopes that Bertie would move in with him again, they were dashed when she upped sticks with their three children and took them off to Belfast where she still had family. With no concerts scheduled for 1966, Joe decided to fly to America to meet up with Betty and young Joseph. He was later to claim that during this visit he and Betty had patched up their differences and were planning to re-start their lives together.

If this was indeed the case and Bertie got wind of it, it might explain why out of the blue she decided to resurrect her previous claim for damages that Joe thought he had heard the last of some three years earlier.

The case reopened in the Dublin High Court on Tuesday 21 February 1967. The public's appetite for scandal was whetted by headlines in Irish newspapers: 'Belfast Woman's Action Against Josef Locke' in *The Irish Independent* and 'Ex-Model's Action Against Singer' in *The Irish Examiner*. Much was made of Bertie being a 'twenty-nine year old model'. There were lengthy press accounts of the court proceedings, with *verbatim* reports of the testimonies of both parties. Private letters written by one or other in the months after the incident were read out in court, and formed the basis for cross-examination. The break-up of Joe's relationship with Bertie Agnew was picked over and revealed to the world in excruciating detail.

The trial lasted three days. Counsel for Bertie claimed that she had been 'assaulted, battered and beaten' by Joe. In reply, Joe's counsel pleaded 'justifiable self-defence', saying that the 'scuffle' had lasted for no more than fifteen seconds, during which Bertie was 'quite hysterical' and had done 'a lot of shouting'. Although it was conceded that Joe had fallen on top of her causing her injury, he was said to be attempting to get a second saucepan, which she was about to throw at him, out of her hands. Joe himself had sustained 'a right crack on the skull' and 'a slit in his head'. And so it went on – claims met by counter-claims, accusations by Bertie of vicious assault and pleas on Joe's behalf that he was simply acting to defend himself.

The family holiday in spring 1963 and letters Bertie had written while abroad came under close scrutiny. Joe said that he had hoped that the Spanish sunshine might help Bertie recover from her injuries. Bertie responded that he had an ulterior motive for the holiday: to try to persuade her to withdraw the assault charge against him. While there, she said, he put pressure on her to write letters to the court saying that she now considered that the matter had been as much her fault as Joe's; that it was in essence 'a purely domestic affair;' and that she would not be returning for any court proceedings. These letters were addressed to District Justice Molony in Dublin early in 1963, but Bertie now claimed that the letters were dictated to her by Joe and were the 'price she had to pay for her ticket to Canada'.

Joe faced some awkward questions about his current marital status and his previous marriages. But the real-life courtroom drama came when a letter dated 1963, from Betty to Bertie (the two women in Joe's life), was read out in court. Betty pulled no punches in her abuse of Joe, calling him 'vermin', and assured her that she (Betty) would readily give Joe his divorce if only he would return their son to her in California. In the face of this emphatic denunciation, the court was astonished to hear from Joe that he and Betty were now reconciled and that there were no plans for them to divorce.

In his summing up and direction to the jury the Judge was even-handed: the accounts given by the two parties were contradictory, and the members of the jury must decide for themselves whose testimony, Joe's or Bertie's, they found more credible. In reference to possible damages he took what would strike many today as a quaintly – or outrageously – condescending line: "Ladies are notoriously proud of their legs and anything which happened to them was an upset...It was perhaps of more importance for a young lady than for an elderly woman." Where the jury's sympathies lay was clear enough from their awarding Bertie £2,560 compensation with costs.

Limbo in Dublin

The conclusion of the court case left Joe in a kind of limbo. Despite what he had said in court, his marriage to Betty was irrevocably over, as was his relationship with Bertie. Betty was in California with her son and Bertie back in Belfast with her three children, where Joe, with a UK warrant out for his arrest over his tax affairs, couldn't visit them. He was down to a handful of singing engagements and once more living the life of a single man.

We get some sense of what his life was like at this period from the historian Roy Foster who was then an undergraduate at Trinity College. He had taken a flat, 'a rambling place perched high up' in the Corn Exchange, and thus had Joe as his landlord. Foster recalls him paying nocturnal visits to the building. Joe's yellow E-Type Jaguar was often left 'rakishly up on the pavement outside.' One evening he called at Foster's flat, mistaking it for one belonging to one of his lady-friends, and was beginning, "The name's Locke, *Josef* Locke." Then, realizing his mistake, he stumbled off down the corridor, swaying slightly as he walked. On another occasion, when Foster was leaving for a morning lecture, he discovered Joe fast asleep in the car. He remembers him as 'an imposing figure in his loud check jacket, canary waistcoat and silk cravat'.

Meanwhile in England...

It was at this lowest point in Joe's personal life and singing career that events across the water took a surprising turn that was to bring him once more to public attention in the very theatres and clubs in the English provinces where he had made his reputation twenty years before.

A singer called Erik Ellison, London-born but of Norwegian parents, had a strong tenor voice similar in tone and range to Joe's. It was so similar that many people were convinced that he was Joe, but performing under a different name. What fed the illusion was that Ellison was physically quite like Joe, tall and strongly built, with a round

English Tenor Erik Ellison aka 'Mr X' in his prime, impersonating Josef Locke

smiling face and twinkling eyes. Among those deceived by the resemblance were the police and the Inland Revenue, who made a raid on Ellison's dressing room when he was performing in the Theatre Club in Accrington in the belief that he was the absconding singer, and were only persuaded otherwise when he produced his driving licence and other documents.

This case of mistaken identity alerted Ellison to the possibility of trading upon his resemblance to Joe by re-branding himself as 'Mr. X', and letting people think that he might be Josef Locke performing under an alias. As 'Mr. X' he appeared on Hughie Green's *Opportunity Knocks* television show, and he followed this up by securing a booking for a season in Blackpool.[4]

When news of his *doppelganger* got back to Joe in Ireland, he was at first wryly amused, "I hope he pays my tax then too." But then he must have reflected that if someone could build a career out of looking like Josef Locke and borrowing his repertoire, then there might still be an audience in England for the real thing. Nothing was happening for him in Ireland, his fiftieth birthday had just passed, and he was living on his own. Might it finally be time for him to return to Blackpool and face the music?

---

[4] *In 1975 'Mr X' took his impersonations of Josef a step further and released his own recordings of 'Violetta' and Galway Bay'.*

CHAPTER EIGHT

The Returning Hero
1967-1975

Decision Time

The entertainment scene in England that Joe was returning to in the autumn of 1967 was very different from the one he had left behind nine years earlier. Variety was all but dead. Instead of the familiar twice-nightly medleys of popular song, comic acts, performing dogs, acrobats, and musical novelties, 1960s audiences wanted something slicker and more sophisticated, something that aped the stylishness of the shows they saw nightly on their television-sets and was closer musically to the world of the pop charts. The Moss theatre chain had severed its links with music hall and by the mid-1960s most of its city centre theatres had been closed and the sites sold off to developers. It was in the clubs, nightclubs and working men's clubs of different kinds, that the old stars of variety were now making a living, and it was in these new, more intimate surroundings that Joe's career was to gain its second wind.

In Ireland something like the old-style variety show survived for a little longer. Joe was able in the 1970s to put together *The Josef Locke Show*, a music hall entertainment blending comedy acts and dancing girls, centred around himself as host, singing and telling stories and keeping up a constant flow of patter. It ran in Dublin and Cork and Limerick and attracted full houses every night.

In these years, too, a profound change was to come over Joe's private life. Whereas by the late 1960s his private life was a shambles, with three failed marriages and one stormy long-term relationship behind him, and six, if not seven, surviving children by four (or five) different women, he was to meet in Carmel Dignam someone who would be a calming influence on his life and share his interests; and finally bring to an end the series of self-destructive relationships that Joe seemed drawn to like a moth to a flame.

Facing the Music

Before Joe could resume his career in England he had first to come to a settlement with the Inland Revenue. There was still a warrant out for his arrest from the Bankruptcy Court in Blackpool, so he contacted the Court and announced his intention of returning to England and sorting out his debts. Joe returned to Blackpool on Wednesday 20 September 1967 and duly appeared before the Registrar Mr. G.N.P.

'Court music may not be so sweet'

—REGISTRAR

THE Blackpool Bankruptcy Court Registrar (Mr G. N. P. White) yesterday warned Irish tenor Josef Locke that there would be very considerable and grave consequences if he did not appear again on December 20 to face his public examination.

White the next day. White had been Joe's solicitor some years earlier and would have known the defaulting singer better than most, but for the moment the formalities of their respective situations were observed.

Joe apologised to the Court for absconding, but said that he had been in Ireland at the time of the last court session and "did not remember receiving the notice of the hearing." The first part of this was certainly true: Joe was in Ireland on the day of the last hearing when the warrant for his arrest was issued. As for him not receiving the notice sent to him by registered post, that was harder to explain away, but the Registrar chose not to pursue the matter. Joe also pleaded, by way of extenuation, that he had had 'a sort of nervous breakdown' around that time.

The hearing was relatively short. The Registrar accepted Joe's apology but ordered him to appear again before the Court on 20 December. In the meantime he was to make payments of £150 for every week he was working. He was warned of the grave consequences that would follow if he failed to turn up for further public examination in December. On 20 December Joe appeared before the Registrar again. He had by this time paid £1,500 towards the settlement of his debts and he asked for the weekly sum of £150 to be reduced. This was not agreed to: instead he was told he would have to appear before the Court at regular intervals until the amount owing to the Inland Revenue – by now estimated at £11,000 – had been paid off.

It was reported in the press that, on coming out of the court, Joe turned up Church Street to the ABC Cinema (the old Hippodrome theatre) where he was a singing 'Father Christmas' to a party of 400 pensioners. His opening number was 'Pack up your troubles in your old kit bag, and smile, smile, smile…', and perhaps he did feel, with the threat of arrest removed, that he had finally packed up his troubles and could afford to smile. His run-in with the Inland Revenue certainly didn't do him any harm with the general public. He was later to say, "It's the one thing you can be wanted for in this country and [still] be a hero in the eyes of the people."

Out of the Frying Pan

However any relief that Joe felt at the threat of arrest in England being lifted from him must have must have been tempered by the knowledge that he was now in legal hot water back in Ireland.

The circumstances were these. The day after his first appearance at the Bankruptcy Court in Blackpool, Joe had gone to the Companies Registration Office in Dublin Castle, where he asked to examine the file dealing with his ownership of the Corn Exchange Building on Burgh Quay. He removed a number of documents, listing, he later said, the nominal directors of the company – members of his family with no financial interest in the company – and substituted a revised list he had made up beforehand. The former documents he took away with him and burned at the Burgh Quay that evening.

The removal of the documents was noticed almost immediately by office staff who reported it to the Gardaí. With the result that around midnight they went to Joe's home in Greystones, arrested him, charged him with theft and took him into custody. Having spent the night in a police cell, he appeared in court the following day and was released on bail. When the case finally came up at the Dublin District Court on 16 November Joe pleaded not guilty to the charge of theft, saying that he had removed the documents quite openly, believing them to be his own property, and not – as was legally the case – the property of the Registration Office. There was no intention to defraud and no person other than himself had a financial interest in the company. At no point had he attempted to conceal or deny what he had done. However the judge in the case was not impressed, said the defendant should have known he was doing something illegal, and sentenced him to four months imprisonment, which Joe gave notice he would appeal.

The matter hung over Joe for a year until 12 November 1968 when the appeal against the sentence was finally considered at the Circuit Court. The conviction of the District Court was upheld but, instead of a prison sentence, Joe was fined £50, a meagre enough sum that he could easily afford, albeit presumably leaving him with a criminal conviction against his name.

Back in Harness

Despite these court appearances on each side of the Irish Sea, the surprising thing is how quickly Joe slipped back into his old busy routine of appearances across the north of England. In the last week of September he came on as a last-minute substitute for Ruby Murray at Club 99 in Barrow-in-Furness, and then the following week he was at two other clubs, the La Scala near Doncaster and the Ba-Ba Club in Barnsley. Through October and into December he was in cabaret at the Mersey Hotel in Didsbury; the

Casino Club, Burnley; the La Strada, Sunderland; Allinson's Theatre Club, Liverpool; the Savoy Club, Wakefield; the Ritz Theatre Club, Brighouse; and the Starlight Club, Blackburn.

Then it was back to Northern Ireland on 11 December 1967 to co-star with comedian Frank Carson in a week's run at the Grove Theatre on Belfast's Shore Road, his first appearance north of the border since 1954. Joe was accompanied by Derek Marsden on the Hammond Organ, and there was a chorus-line of 'Balmoral Lassies' – Balmoral in Belfast, presumably, rather than Balmoral on Deeside – who were promised to 'Dance to your Delight'. It's a safe bet, since this was Belfast in the 1960s, that they were more modestly costumed than the Blackpool girls Joe was familiar with in the 1950s.

In England once more, Joe had top billing in the pantomime *Mother Goose* in the Oldham Empire. On this occasion he was the show's producer as well as singing in it. It opened on Saturday 23 December 1967, with the usual two shows daily until Saturday 6 January   Christmas Day excluded. A sign of the times was that Joe was now appearing alongside television and radio stars, Bobby Bennett from *Opportunity Knocks* and Tony Prince of Radio Caroline, rather than with variety artists as in the past.

Joe received many telegrams from his Showbusiness friends to welcome him back to Blackpool, including this spoof telegram purporting to be from 'The Taxman'. (Courtesy of Mrs. Geraldine McCallion)

'The Clubland Phenomenon'

It was a notable change from Joe's earlier period in England that he was now rarely performing in theatres. Indeed most of the theatres he had sung at in the 1940s and 1950s, including those of Moss Empire theatre chain, had closed, been converted to cinemas, were lying derelict or had their sites sold off to developers. Joe was almost exclusively to be heard in clubs, hotels and the grander sort of public houses. With the exception of the affectionate parody of the Edwardian music hall in television's *The Good Old Days* – the name of which says it all – the audiences for variety were just not there any more.

Cabaret, on the other hand, was a different matter. Although its modern origins lay in the 1880s and it was in vogue in the inter-war period, it had successfully renewed itself in the post-war years and in the 1960s still had a large popular following. The natural venue for this new kind of entertainment was in the clubs that were springing up all over the country. It was a format which played to Joe's strengths, his easy stage presence and his ability to interact with his audience, joke with them and win them over. The more intimate atmosphere was also ideally suited to Joe's way of putting over a song, and, when combined with the use of a microphone, helped make up for any loss of natural power in his voice.

Joe's success in the clubs can be gauged from the glowing reviews he received. In May 1968, *The Stage* reported that, "Clubland's current bill-topping phenomenon is undoubtedly Josef Locke... Don't believe anyone who says the voice isn't as good as it used to be. It just isn't true… Locke is a great artist in every respect."

We have already noted the list of nightclubs visited by Joe in the autumn of 1967. To these we can add others where he appeared in spring 1968: the Talk of the North Club in Eccles, the Cresta Club in Birmingham, the Ace of Clubs in Worksop, Tito's Club in Cardiff; and a succession of other clubs across the north of England. In May he even managed to fit in a Sunday show for Val Parnell at the London Palladium, and on 23 June an all-day Charity Gala at Manchester's Belle Vue. Singing in the clubs was certainly not as exhausting as singing twice-nightly, six-days-a-week in variety, but it was still a demanding schedule.

Blackpool Once Again

Late in June 1968 Joe made his re-appearance on Blackpool's Golden Mile for the first time in ten years when he topped the bill in the summer season show at the Queen's Theatre. *The Queen's Show*, directed by Dick Hurran, featured the Kaye Sisters, Freddie Davies, The Three Bizzarros, Mike Newman, the Tiller Girls and Johnny Hart. Joe had the prime spot at the end of the show. His popularity with the Blackpool public seemed undimmed by his long period away. The theatre was filled night after night, it was said, "to the extent of breaking the all-time records for that hall."

This was despite Blackpool in 1968 being a very different place from the town Joe had

JOSEF LOCKE

Josef himself writes . . .

His first appearance in England was at the end of the War, at Victoria Palace, London in 1945.

This is his twelfth Blackpool season where he has played every theatre in town, opening the Queens with his own show in 1953—He named the theatre 'QUEENS' for the late Jimmy Brennan, a great friend of Joe's.

For years he was the best selling singer on Columbia Records, and has now a new L.P. just released called "Hear my Song" on the "Music for Pleasure" label.

Standing 6ft. 2ins., and now is almost three stones lighter than ten years ago, he enjoys his singing better than ever.

Josef has sung in almost every country in the world and will be glad to sing any requests made by the Audience, who he hopes will fully enjoy the excellent 1968 Queens Show.

Joe 'reintroduces' himself to Blackpool audiences in the programme for the 1968 Queen's Show, his first summer season in the town since 1958. (Author's own collection)

last performed in in 1958. Of the vast numbers of holidaymakers who had once filled its hotels and boarding houses in the summer months, thousands were now venturing further afield on package holidays to Spanish resorts like Benidorm and Magaluf.

There was change, too, in the musical landscape. The mid-1960s was the heyday of the 'Liverpool Sound' or Merseybeat – the Beatles, Gerry and the Pacemakers, Cilla Black, and Billy J. Kramer and the Dakotas – and this was mirrored in the Blackpool summer season shows of the period. Cliff Richard and the Shadows topped the bill in the new ABC Cinema's (former Hippodrome's) summer show *Holiday Carnival* in 1963. The Beatles gave a series of Sunday concerts at different venues in Blackpool from July to September of the same year; and again in 1964. The Dave Clark Five were in *The Dick Emery Show* at the Winter Gardens for the summer of 1964; Gerry and the Pacemakers at the South Pier's summer season show in 1965; and Billy J. Kramer and the Dakotas at the same venue's summer show in 1966. Cilla Black appeared with the Dublin group, the Bachelors, in the ABC Cinema's 1966 summer show *Holiday Startime*; and topped the bill in the 1969 version of the show three years later.

That Joe was able to hold his own and draw crowds in the era of *Top of The Pops* and the chart-ratings speak volumes for the affection in which he was still held by the Blackpool public. On 3 August, along with Ken Dodd, Les Dawson and other artists performing in Blackpool that summer, he took part in *The Blackpool Show* broadcast on BBC Radio 2. And, true to form, he combined his Queen's Theatre appearances with other Sunday night performances from July to September in the Winter Gardens in Morecambe. It was at one of these Sunday night concerts that Joe suddenly recognized fellow Derry man Willie Loughlin in the audience. Hailing him from the stage, Joe dragged Willie up to join him in an impromptu duet.

It helped that Joe was in good shape physically and mentally. Whereas in the mid-1950s he had been around eighteen stone, overweight even for someone with his bulky 6' 2" frame – so much so that the *Sunderland Daily Echo* once described him unflatteringly as 'that mountain of a singer from Ireland' – he had successfully shed three stone and was something closer to his 'fighting weight', not a phrase to be used lightly in Joe's case. He was also slowly sorting out his personal life. He was on the way to securing a divorce from Betty in California, the price being that he agreed to his son Joseph living permanently with his mother. The split with Bertie Agnew was also final, although the loose ends of that relationship called him back to Belfast in the summer of 1968, when a question arose about the maintenance payment for their three children, which Joe had been paying by cheque directly to Bertie instead of through the family courts, as he was required to do.

Throughout the autumn and winter months of 1968-69 Joe was in cabaret performing in clubs across the north of England. He had a run at the Pavilion Theatre in Glasgow in late March 1969, and even managed a couple of engagements in Ireland, at The Orchard in Bandon, County Cork in December 1968 and at the Talk of the Town in Belfast in early May.

An Old Pal

In July 1969 Joe was back at the Queen's Theatre, following up on his success of the previous summer. This time his co-stars were Jimmy Clitheroe, Bobby Bennett, the Dallas Boys and Alan Randal. The Tiller Girls and an acrobat troupe completed the lineup, supported by The Queen's Singers and the resident orchestra.

He was accompanied on piano by James MacCafferty, his old friend from Derry, whom Joe had persuaded to join him for the summer in Blackpool. MacCafferty was a multi-talented musician with a long and distinguished history as a choir-master.[1] He had played too as accompanist in concerts Joe had given in Derry in the 1940s, and they enjoyed a close personal and musical rapport. However their work schedule through that Blackpool summer was a gruelling one. Apart from the two shows a night six days a week, the pair often flew to the Isle of Man on Sundays to do shows in Douglas as well. And there were additional late night cabaret slots in Blackpool.

MacCafferty may have been an old friend, but the pecking order between the two was clear enough. While Joe now was earning about £1,000 a week, his accompanist was paid a less than princely £50 a week for his services. He was also, if accounts are to be believed, put up at a middling Blackpool hotel while Joe lived in style in a much grander establishment.

From MacCafferty we learn how Joe's part of the programme went. He mostly sang the old songs for which he was well known: 'Violetta', 'Le Rêve Passe', and 'I'll Take you Home Again, Kathleen'. Often he prompted the audience to sing along with him, which they were happy to do. After 'The Holy City' he would call for "a drop of the holy water", and a glass of Bull's Eye Brown Ale would be brought on stage for him, which led into 'The Drinking Song' from *The Student Prince*. Throughout he spiced his act with humour, and got a laugh when he introduced the musicians in the pit as "Sir Thomas Beecham and all his little pills." He sang a song from his latest recording 'How Small We Are' to an arrangement by MacCafferty and the two of them sang a duet together, 'The Bold Gendarmes'. Always the closing song was 'Goodbye', Joe hitting the top notes with his customary ease.

Yet that summer was an anxious time for the two Derry men. 'The Troubles', which had started almost a year before with the Civil Rights March in Derry in October 1968, erupted again on 12 August 1969 after an Apprentice Boys' March in the city. The resulting 'Battle of the Bogside' brought violence and chaos on to Derry's streets. Each evening after the Blackpool shows, the two men grimly watched the news on television, as the violence took hold and spread to Belfast and other towns.

---

[1] *MacCafferty's children's choir, The Little Gaelic Singers had toured the United States in the 1950s and an adult choir, The MacCafferty Singers, was to reach the final of the BBC's Choir of the Year competition in 1984.*

As sung by Josef Locke in the Bulls Eye Brown TV Commercial

Joe, glass and bottle in hand, adorns the sheet music of the song from his television commercial for ale in the later 1960s.

The TV Celebrity

The introduction of Bull's Eye Brown Ale to Joe's stage act was shrewdly calculated. Joe was no ale drinker himself, but, alert as ever to the possibilities of turning an extra penny, he had broken into the world of television advertising and was the singing voice promoting Bull's Eye Brown Ale, a local brew. Joe sang the advert's jingle "If you want to get your whistle wet then go for a Bull's Eye Brown" to the tune of Stephen Foster's 'Oh Susanna'.[2]

Before 1958 Joe had made a number of appearances on television, but always as a singer in variety. What was different in the late 1960s is that he began to be invited on to television programmes as a celebrity. His first appearance of this kind was in June 1969 as a guest artist on Bob Monkhouse's game show *The Golden Shot*. This was followed a few weeks later by his being the guest of Mike and Bernie Winters on ITV's *Mike and Bernie's Show*. These appearances involved little in the way of preparation or rehearsal and yet paid much more than a single live stage show. They also provided invaluable publicity for his latest records.

Now that Joe was back in England, he was able to resume his recording career which had been in abeyance during his years in Ireland. There was a spate of new recordings in the summer of 1969: 'How Small We Are'; 'Danny Boy' (surprisingly for the first time); 'Edelweiss'; 'Try a Little Tenderness'; 'Little Altar Boy'; 'Marta'; 'The Last Waltz'. They were released by Decca as an LP, *The World of Josef Locke Today*. Some of these recordings, to be frank, are not among Joe's best. 'Little Altar Boy', with its over-lush orchestral accompaniment and mawkish lyrics, must be among the worst. He was on surer ground singing from his Irish repertoire. Commenting on another album issued at this time, *A Song of Ireland*, a reviewer in *The Hi-Fi News and Record Review* found much to praise, albeit with a sting in the tail: "With the benefit of modern recording and singing with tasteful restraint, Josef Locke has matured into a fine interpreter of McCormack style material, such as 'Macushla', 'Rose of Tralee' and 'The Bard of Armagh' and even manages to make 'Galway Bay' sound quite acceptable."

The Royal Albert Hall and David Bowie

Early in 1970 a number of Irish customers and the management of Mooney's pub opposite The Savoy Hotel in London decided to organize a charity concert for the National Society for Mentally Handicapped Children (MENCAP) and St. Patrick's Island Building Fund. Not ones for half measures, they hired the Royal Albert Hall for Thursday 12 March and engaged a notable line-up of performers, at the head of which were Joe and the Ken Mackintosh Orchestra. Actress Maureen O'Sullivan, the Irish folk band the Johnstons, and Butty Sugrue, the Irish strongman, were among other artists appearing. Joe and Butty's paths had crossed years earlier when both were touring Ireland in the early 1940s, Joe with Jimmy O'Dea and Butty with Duffy's Circus, but

[2] *In later years, when he was back in Ireland, Joe sang in a well-known television advertisement for The Irish Permanent Building Society.*

on this occasion Joe seems not to have realized Butty was on the bill. "There I was, in white tie and tails, in the middle of 'La Donna é Mobile' when on walked Butty dressed like Goliath pulling a motor-cycle behind him. And the motor-cyclist was trying to ride the bike in the opposite direction." (After the Albert Hall Show, the two men kept in touch and on New Year's Eve 1975 Joe was the guest star at the opening of Butty's new nightclub in Kilburn.)

One of the support acts at the Albert Hall that night was a quiet young man David Bowie, who had yet to make a name for himself. Singer-guitarist Richard Hensey, who recalled the occasion, remembered that during rehearsals Bowie asked Joe for his autograph; and, when Joe asked whether it was for his mum, he said, no, it was for himself – an unexpected and oddly touching tribute from one who was later to become a very different sort of showbusiness phenomenon.

The March 1970 concert in London's Royal Albert Hall in which Joe appeared alongside the then, relatively unknown David Bowie.

Last Blackpool Seasons

In summer 1970 Joe was scheduled to appear on Blackpool Central Pier alongside Al Read, Nat Jackley and Lena Martell in a show that was to run for eleven weeks, from 9 July until 26 September. But a fortnight into the run he sustained a back injury that kept him out of the show for the remainder of the season. (There were rumours locally at the time that Joe and Al Read had 'a punch-up' on the Blackpool seafront, in which Joe was injured.)

While recuperating in Dublin Joe was once again able to turn his attention to his property dealings. The Corn Exchange Building on Burgh Quay, which he had bought in partnership with others for about £40,000 in 1961 and which had got Joe into trouble with the Companies Registration Office, was finally sold in November 1970 for – it was reported – about £200,000. The buyers, Vico Investments Ltd, planned to demolish the building and replace it with an office block, although their planning application was subsequently turned down and the building still stands on the Burgh Quay. Joe denied categorically in the newspapers that he owned the building, but *The Irish Independent* was unconvinced: "[Joe] should know by now that that Irish have a knack of only believing things when they are denied."

The following month, on 8 December [1970], Joe took part in a *Night of Memories* concert at the Guildhall in Derry organized by St. Mary's Boys' Club. It was a remarkable event that brought together for the first and only time successive generations of Derry musicians from 'Wee Willie' Doherty (b. 1890), James MacCafferty, Joe and Michael O'Duffy (b. 1915, 1917 and 1918 respectively); Patrick O'Hagan (b. 1920s), Phil Coulter and Majella Brady (b. 1940s); to Peter Boy/Roddy (of the Trend) and Eurovision winner Dana (b. 1950s). But it was Joe, coming on stage close to midnight, who provided the fitting finale, "with a performance redolent of the days when his powerful recordings of 'Goodbye' and 'Violetta' were sweeping the world."

One might have thought that, at almost 54, Joe's days of overseas touring were behind him. But early in January 1971 it was reported in the Irish press that he was shortly to be leaving for a three week season singing in clubs in Hong Kong. Whether anything came of this, we don't know. He did, however, fly to Canada in May 1971 where he recorded a number of guest appearances on a popular Toronto television show set in an imaginary English pub *The Pig and Whistle* that were broadcast later that year.

Joe was originally booked to appear on Blackpool's North Pier for the summer months of 1971 in *Showtime*, a Bernard Delfont production, with Jimmy Clitheroe, Freddie and the Dreamers, Ken Goodwin and others. This would have earned him, he reckoned, £25,000. Yet again, however, Joe had to pull out just as the show was due to open, suffering from a slipped disc. He was never again to appear in a Blackpool summer show.

The injury to Joe, if not exactly fortuitous, left him free to return to Ireland and to the new woman who had recently come into his life.

The Derry artistes photographed on the evening of 'The Night of Memories' concert in December 1970, including Phil Coulter (bottom row, 1st right), Dana (bottom row, 2nd right), James MacCafferty (middle row, 1st right) and Joe (bottom row, 1st left).

Carmel Dignam

In 1966 Joe had advertised for a secretary who could double as a groom for the horses in his stud farm at Kilcoole, County Wicklow. The successful applicant was a young woman from Celbridge, County Kildare, Carmel Dignam, who had been a working pupil in the stables at Castletown House, home of the Connolly-Carew family. (In the 1960s Diana Connolly-Carew and her brother Patrick, the younger generation of the family, were outstanding show-jumping riders who represented Ireland in the Olympics.) In Carmel Joe was to find someone who not only shared his love of horses and the country, but a friend and loving companion who was to become his wife. Their marriage would last until Joe's death in 1999.

The first the public knew about Carmel and Joe was the announcement of their engagement in the Social and Personal Column of *The Irish Times* on 5 August 1971, when the couple were holidaying together in Spain. They had become engaged some weeks before, but had managed to keep it quiet until the official press notice. The wedding followed within a week: the new Mr. and Mrs. McLaughlin being married in Chesterfield Registry Office in Derbyshire on Thursday 12 August. It was Joe's third (legal) marriage, and Carmel's first. After the signing of the register, they left immediately for Ireland, where Lord and Lady Carew, her former employers, provided

Joe and Carmel Dignam on their wedding day in Chesterfield on Thursday 12 August 1971. (By kind permission of the McLaughlin family)

a wedding reception for them at Castletown House. There were other receptions, including a lively one that Joe organized for his friends in The Royal Starlight Hotel in Bray.

The Bogside Tour

The first few months of their married life Joe spent quietly with Carmel at their Kilcoole stud farm. But events in Derry on 'Bloody Sunday', 30 January 1972, when British army paratroops shot 26 unarmed civilians taking part in a peaceful protest march against internment, killing 14 of them, shattered their rural calm. Joe, a Derry man to the core, was deeply affected and travelled north to attend the funeral of the victims in St. Mary's Church in the Creggan. Then, keen to do something practical, he headed up a concert three weeks later in the National Stadium in Dublin in aid of the families of those who had been shot by the soldiers. All the participating artists performed for free.

He returned to Derry the following week to take part in the so-called 'Bogside Tour' organized by St. Mary's Boys' Club: a series of concerts in Derry and across the border in Donegal in clubs and dance-halls to raise money for the victims' families and those of internees. He was joined in the concerts by local Derry soprano Maureen Hegarty, James MacCafferty on piano, and the Nazareth Ceili Band.

The first concerts were in Derry's Creggan Estate and in Lourdes Hall on 27 and 28 February. They were followed by concerts on successive evenings in Ballybofey, Carndonagh, Donegal Town, Buncrana, Gortahork, and Letterkenny, and a final two concerts back in Creggan Estate on the 11 and 12 March: eleven concerts in the space of fourteen days. This was not the first time that Joe had given his support to charitable causes in his home town. (He had a history of performing for good causes that went back to his first concert in Derry's Guildhall in 1942.) On this 1972 tour Joe made no political statements, and indeed he was once quoted as saying that he had no interest whatsoever in politics; but his involvement in the Bogside Tour was a powerful

The Derry Journal, Friday 25th February, 1972

10

ST. MARY'S BOYS' CLUB PROMOTIONS

VARIETY CONCERT JOSEF LOCKE

starring

BOGSIDE CHARITY TOUR

Sunday, 27th Feb.
CREGGAN ESTATE

Monday, 28th Feb.
LOURDES HALL

Wed., 1st March
BUTT HALL
Ballybofey

Thurs., 2nd March
BORDERLAND
Muff

Fri., 3rd March
LILAC
Carndonagh

Sunday, 5th March
PAVESI
Donegal Town

Wed., 8th March
PLAZA
Buncrana

Thurs., 9th March
CORTAHORK HALL

Fri., 10th March
FIESTA
Letterkenny

Sun., 12th March
CREGGAN ESTATE

SCENE
CATHY MURRAY
LOCAL IRISH DANCE TROUPE
MÍCHÍ & NOEL
McCAFFERTY GROUP
DON McCAFFERTY — JOSIE McINTYRE
HUBERT HAMILTON
WEE WILLIE

MAUREEN HEGARTY

BIG JOE

Also appearing : NAZARETH HOUSE CEILI BAND
AILEACH FOLK
CEOL na RÍ

Compere: Mr. Harry Reddy
At the Piano : James McCafferty, George Doherty

SUNDAY NIGHT'S CONCERT IS COMPLETELY SOLD OUT. ADMISSION BY TICKET ONLY. SEATS MUST BE CLAIMED BEFORE 8.30 p.m. NO STANDING.

On behalf of S.M.B.C. I wish to thank sincerely—Josef Locke and all the artistes and the Hall Proprietors for giving their services to this Charity Show free of Charge.

J. P. CAROLAN, CC

The February/March 'Bogside Tour' of Derry and Donegal in which Joe was the chief attraction. He was commonly called 'Big Joe' by his friends and fellow-performers in Ireland.

expression of solidarity with his fellow townspeople at this darkest of times for the city.

This was the start of Joe's days singing with Maureen Hegarty, who was to become his favoured duet partner in Northern Ireland for the next ten years or so, particularly at shows around Derry and Donegal.

Around this time Joe realized a dream he had had for some time of buying a farm in Donegal. It was at Burnfoot, a small village, just over the border from Derry. Given the political convulsions within Northern Ireland, it had the advantage for Joe of being within easy reach of the city and allowing him to visit friends and give concerts there, without having to suffer the constant alarms and restrictions that Derry residents now had to live with from day to day.

Old Time Memories and *The Josef Locke Show*

In 1972 Joe was talking of cutting down on his public performances. He had not appeared in England since his marriage, he was fifty-five years old, and it wouldn't have been surprising if he was looking forward to easing up. Carmel and he seemed settled with their two homes in Donegal and Wicklow and press reports frequently reported his purchase of this or that promising mare for their stables.

And yet the lure of the footlights kept drawing him back. At the start of May he began a fortnight's run at Dublin's Olympia Theatre of *Old Time Memories*, described as a 'magical, mirthful musical miscellany'. There was a nod to the 1970s in a pop number by the Brannigans, a Dublin trio; Hal Roach supplied the mirth; but it was Joe in the second half of the show who stirred the memories of his audience and gave them what they had come to hear. "The songs, and (Joe) with them, were all there, taking over the stage and brooking no half-hearted response, right up to the end... [when] 'Goodbye' brought down the house and the curtain." Joe took the show for a week to the Savoy Theatre in Limerick at the end of the month, and then to the Cork Opera House in the second week in June. The review in the *Irish Examiner* echoed those in the Dublin press: "Bravo Josef Locke and thank you for bringing to Cork a night of nights... his rich tenor voice filled every corner of the house and his range is truly that of a master." Audience attendances, too, were impressive: over 15,000 people came to the twelve nights at the Olympia – a box-office record for the theatre – and Cork's 1,000-seater Opera House sold out in advance for the entire week. Joe had always been popular in Ireland, but he seemed now to have acquired something of the status of a national treasure.

Then at the start of November what was substantially the same show as in the spring, but renamed *The Josef Locke Show*, opened at the Olympia Theatre. It was very much the same mixture as before and with many of the same support artists – Deirdre O'Callaghan on harp and the Brannigans – but with Joe as the chief draw, "like a Colossus, dwarfing all that went before." And again for the three weeks of the run the theatre was packed out night after night.

Slowing the Pace

Joe's life by 1973-74 had settled into a familiar routine. He made occasional personal appearances in cabaret or at charity events around Ireland. There were fewer theatre appearances: two weeks of *The Josef Locke Show* in the Cork Opera House in June 1973 and again in June 1974; four weeks of the show in Dublin's Olympia in June-July 1973 and two weeks at the same venue in May 1974. The support acts were different in the different versions of the show, but the common factor and star attraction was Joe himself, now often dubbed 'Mr Showbusiness' in the advance publicity as if he were the very embodiment of the spirit of variety. Most of his time, however, seems to have been spent at home with Carmel. In October 1972 he had bought The Orchard Inn in Greystones for £60,000 in her name, planning to turn it into a steakhouse, with Carmel, who was described in one newspaper as a 'cordon bleu chef and a qualified company secretary', presumably inked in as manager. Between the farm and the stables and this new business venture Joe and Carmel must have had their hands full.

It was about the Orchard Inn that Joe told the following story. The local council was being slow about granting him planning permission for an extension to the restaurant. At the same time the councillors were always pestering him for free tickets to his shows at the Gaiety Theatre. One night Joe spotted four black men in the theatre audience and had Gaiety staff invite them to the bar for a drink after the show, knowing the councillors would be there. When they saw Joe drinking with the four, they asked him who they were, and he said they were interested in buying the restaurant, and, since development possibilities seemed to be stalled, he (Joe) was thinking of selling to them. The councillors, as Joe had foreseen, were aghast, and planning permission was magically granted a few weeks later.

Joe made a number of appearances on Irish television. Some of these were hour-long broadcasts from the theatres where *The Josef Locke Show* was playing. On one of these occasions at the Cork Opera House Maureen Hegarty was appearing with Joe. Taking a break during rehearsals, she went outside for a breath of fresh air, where she was accosted by a young man who propositioned her obscenely. Maureen reported this to Carmel who promptly told Joe. He was fit to be tied, all his protective instincts aroused, and it was only with the greatest difficulty that he could be restrained from taking matters into his own hands – and fists – and going outside to give the man a hiding.

From time to time Joe was an invited guest on informal chat and quiz shows like *The Music Game* that were increasingly part of RTÉ's programming schedules. Joe's easy-going style and quick sense of humour that had endeared him to live audience in theatres and clubs over the years made him a natural for programmes of this kind.

New LPs of his recordings continued to appear and found a ready market. In August 1973 it was *I'll Sing It My Way*, which had new versions of his old standards like 'Blaze Away' and 'I'll Take You Home Again Kathleen' plus new songs like the Frank Sinatra number 'My Way' and 'Let There Be Peace' by veteran Irish lyricist Jimmy Kennedy,

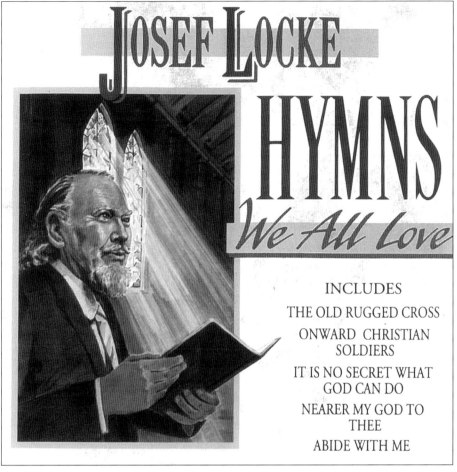

The cover of Joe's 1975 recording 'Hymns We All Love'.

a plea for an end to the violence in the North. It sold an astonishing 10,000 copies in its first week of issue. Also in 1973 a 34-track LP *Singalong* was issued under the Heritage label. And in 1975, at the suggestion of Jimmy Kennedy, Joe recorded an LP of religious hymns, *Hymns We All Love*, a first album from Abergavenny-based Spire Records, with vocal backing from the RTÉ Singers.

Joe's 1974 theatre show received mixed reviews. His co-star in the two-week run at the Olympia theatre in May was Peggy Dell, the veteran singer, pianist and one-time bandleader, who was making a return to the stage in her late-sixties after a decade out of the public eye. The *Irish Times* missed the specialty acts that had formerly added spice to variety, and praised Dell, but found the other musical contributions, including Joe's own – although what the audience had principally come to hear – 'predictable and lacking in spontaneity'. Another reviewer complained that Joe didn't appear on stage until 10.30pm, and found it inexcusable that he should keep the audience waiting for two and a half hours for the star of the show to appear. "That might be all right in cabaret, but not in the theatre."

It was a similar story when the show transferred to the Cork Opera House. Joe himself was in top form, according to the *Irish Examiner*, but the show as whole was mediocre and made 'criminal misuse', that's to say, no effective use at all, 'of the fine stage of the Opera House'. In the writer's view, it could just as well have been put on in a parish hall.

The First Farewell

In the early months of 1975, when Joe and Carmel were back at the farm at Burnfoot, Joe agreed to appear with James MacCafferty's singers and orchestra in three nights of concerts (4, 6 and 7 February) at the Du Pont Club outside Derry in aid of the local Gransha Hospital. Three weeks later, on 26 February, he was involved in another charity concert, this time in Letterkenny, to raise funds for the families of six young fishermen from Burtonport in Donegal who had lost their lives at sea. Joe, like the other artists contributing, gave their services free, but on this occasion it was the band of the Garda Síochána that stole the show: "Rarely will the Fiesta Ballroom (where the concert took place) hear their likes again… It was like 'The Glen Miller Story' reborn."

In mid-April Joe announced that he was retiring from performing in public, and a show at the Royal Dublin Society's premises at Ballsbridge on 29 April with Peggy Dell, and Val Fitzpatrick as compere was advertised as his final appearance. The run-up to the concert was marked by an unseemly row with The Irish Equity Union over a year's unpaid union dues that it claimed Joe owed from the previous year, but which Joe said he had no intention of paying as he would be retiring with immediate effect. However, on the eve of the concert the promoter announced that the fees were being paid, although whether by Joe or by someone else was left unclear, and the concert went ahead as advertised. We don't know how it went, because no reviews that one can discover appeared in the press. Did no one think Josef Locke's 'final appearance' newsworthy? Or had journalists, knowing about the row with Irish Equity, agreed beforehand to boycott the event?

CHAPTER 9

Winding Down
1975-1991

Taking Stock

In the event, the years following Joe's public 'retirement' in April 1975 were not dramatically different from those that had gone before. He undoubtedly spent more time at home with Carmel, either in Donegal or around Dublin, and his new properties demanded his attention. Joe and Carmel shared a love of horses. In the past he had bred racehorses and horses for show-jumping, but at this time they were simply breeding horses for sale. According to Carmel, Joe was no mean horseman himself, although she didn't know where he had picked up his skills, unless (as she once joked) it was riding camels when he was in Egypt.

In spite of his 'final concert' Joe was still being periodically lured out of retirement 'for a few last appearances', many of them for charity. And perhaps because people sensed that this might be their last chance to see him perform in public, these appearances were often booked out in advance. Consequently they served to remind Joe of what he was missing. He summed up his shifting state of mind in a newspaper interview: "When he was on the farm, he was happy and content there – glad that his wild days were over and that he 'was out of the business'. But when he was back on the road, he wished he was back again."

One notable change in his life was that Joe reconnected with his children in England and Ireland, his letters to them showing that, although for obvious reasons he had not always been around when they were small, he had neither forgotten nor lost interest in them. That made it all the harder for him to receive news of the premature death in his twenties of his first son Joseph, who in 1965 had gone to live with his mother in America.[1]

Joe made one well-publicized comeback in 1984, after a number of years when his public performances had dwindled virtually to nothing. But understandably, given his age, his career never recovered the momentum it had in his heyday. There were occasional one-off special appearances at Dublin's new National Concert Hall, at the Cork Opera House – an old favourite of Joe's – and at local festivals of different kinds around the country. But with the exception of a week in Dublin's Olympia in summer

---

[1] Joseph, like his father, had initially chosen a military career, in his case with the U.S. Marines. After leaving the military he married and had a daughter, Candice McLaughlin

Joe photographed in the mid-1970s on his favourite horse, Paddy (By kind permission of the McLaughlin family)

1984, longer runs were now a thing of the past. His only regular performances in these years were in the more intimate atmosphere of the Braemor Rooms at Churchtown, where he shared a singing partnership with soprano Rose Tynan.

The 1980s were a time for looking back and reappraisal. Joe received the Variety Artists' Trust Society's award for his more than four decades' contribution to the variety arts in Ireland, and that was followed by a special edition of Gay Byrne's *Late Late Show* on RTÉ, devoted to Joe and his career.

The Blackpool Centenary Show

If there was a relative lull in Joe's performing post-1975 – and a lull of his own choosing – there were pleasing signs that he had not been forgotten across the Irish Sea. In 1976 Blackpool was celebrating the centenary of the granting of its Royal Charter, which had marked its rise to be the country's northern 'premier' seaside resort. The opening event was a Centenary Command Performance at the Blackpool Opera House on Sunday 25 January. Many of the 'stars' who had appeared on its stages over the years were invited back to perform in the show, resulting in a huge cast of 350, all of whom agreed to waive their fees. Belfast comedian Frank Carson was one of three comperes in what was a five-hour marathon, described in the press as 'Blackpool's glittering Birthday Party'.

EMPIRE THEATRE
OLDHAM

General Manager:
R. MORECAMBE

Telephone:
MAIN 4362

Commencing Saturday, Dec. 23 to Saturday, Jan. 6, 1968
PLEASE NOTE TIMES OF PERFORMANCES

SATURDAY, DEC. 23rd ... 5 p.m. and 8 p.m.	MONDAY, JAN. 1st ... ... 2.15 and 7.15
MONDAY, DEC. 25th ... THEATRE CLOSED	TUESDAY, JAN. 2nd ... ... 2.15 and 7.15
TUESDAY, DEC. 26th ... 2 p.m., 5 p.m., 8 p.m.	WEDNESDAY, JAN. 3rd ... ... 2.15 and 7.15
WEDNESDAY, DEC. 27th ... ... 2.15 and 7.15	THURSDAY, JAN. 4th... ... ... 2.15 and 7.15
THURSDAY, DEC. 28th ... ... 2.15 and 7.15	FRIDAY, JAN. 5th ... ... 2.15 and 7.15
FRIDAY, DEC. 29th ... ... 2.15 and 7.15	SATURDAY, JAN. 6th ... 2 p.m., 5 p.m., 8 p.m.
SATURDAY, DEC. 30th ... 2 p.m., 5 p.m., 8 p.m.	

Philip Bernard presents a traditional "Laughter-Package" Pantomime

ON THE STAGE

WITH GUEST STAR

JOSEF LOCKE
IN

MOTHER GOOSE

WITH

FROM "OPPORTUNITY KNOCKS"	FROM RADIO CAROLINE NORTH
BOBBY BENNETT	**TONY PRINCE**
TOP T.V. IMPRESSIONIST	OLDHAM'S OWN D-J

TWELVE REX GREY GIRLS	FRANK LYNN	SPEED MANIACS FILMED CAR RIDE

Avril Ellis ★ **Betty Wood** ★ **Amanda Birkin**

THE "I DON'T CARE" BOY

JOHNNY DALLAS
AS MOTHER GOOSE

PANTO DIRECTED BY AUBREY PHILLIPS AND PRODUCED BY JOSEF LOCKE

Popular Prices

ORCHESTRA STALLS	8/6 (Child 6/6)
CENTRE STALLS...	6/6 (Child 5/–)
REAR STALLS	4/6 (Child 3/–)
CENTRE CIRCLE	8/6 (Child 6/6)
SIDE CIRCLE	6/6 (Child 5/–)

★ Child Prices NOT applicable Saturdays, Boxing Day or New Year's Day.

Party and Postal Bookings

O.A.P. PARTY RATES TO CERTAIN PERFORMANCES: APPLY BOX OFFICE FOR DETAILS. PARTY AND POSTAL BOOKINGS NOW ACCEPTED. THEATRE BOX OFFICE OPENS FROM NOVEMBER 13th ONWARDS FROM 10 A.M. TO 6 P.M.

Douglas the Printers, 31 Sussex Street, Rhyl, Tel, 3199.

The flier for Joe's appearance in pantomime at Christmas 1967 at the Empire Theatre, Oldham, his first major show in England after his return. He was listed as the 'Guest Star' in Mother Goose, but he had also produced the show.

Joe (extreme right) as the Emperor of China in the 1969 pantomime Aladdin, with co-stars Mike (1st left) and Bernie Winters (3rd left). (Alamy Photographs)

Joe photographed with two well-known local singers on visits home to Derry: with 'Dana' in 1976, and Willie Loughlin in 1981. (By Kind Permission of the Derry Journal)

Joe pictured behind the bar of his Donegal pub at Burnfoot, which he renamed The Mountainy Farmer. This was his fourth - and last time - as a landlord in the licensed trade.

Joe, as his audiences saw him in the 1980s: relaxed onstage and tanned by his frequent trips to the Spanish sun. In these later years of his career, Joe's taste in clothes had moved from sober, sharply-tailored suits to more vibrant and colourful jackets and ties. (Alamy Photographs)

Joe's three children by Bertie Agnew, pictured in the mid-1960s. From left: Peter, Nikki and Karl.

Joe and Carmel celebrate their 25th Wedding Anniversary in August 1996, with Joe's daughter Nikki (centre).

Joe with his grand-son in Spain and at home in the mid-1990s.

Joe photographed in the last few years of his life in Ireland, playing his beloved Challen Baby Grand piano with his grand-daughter alongside.

One of the last public triumphs of Joe's life, when he met Princess Diana at the premiere of the Hear My Song film in March 1992. (Alamy Photographs)

The final resting place of Josef Locke's ashes, in Dublin's Glasnevin Cemetery.

The Centenary Command Performance

At the Opera House, Sunday 25th January 1976

BLACKPOOL

CENTENARY

To Commemorate the Granting to Blackpool of its first Royal Charter and to mark over One Hundred Years as the Entertainment Capital of Europe.

1876 ▬ 1976

Programme for the Blackpool Centenary Show in January 1976.

Joe was one of the celebrities specially invited to lend lustre to the occasion. It had been six years since he had last appeared in Blackpool, but memories of his high and palmy days were obviously still strong. He was given 'top of the bill', with a spot just before the Grand Finale. Even organist Reginald Dixon on the Mighty Wurlitzer – Joe's sometime rival for the title 'Mr. Blackpool' – had to settle for a spot earlier in the programme with his medley of seaside tunes.

When Joe finally came onstage towards the end of the evening, introduced by television actor John Inman, expectations were high. He started off with his old favourites, 'Violetta' and 'Blaze Away', and worked his way through his familiar repertoire, drawing tears from the eyes of many with 'I'll Take You Home Again, Kathleen'. He ended, as always, with 'Goodbye'. The 3000-strong audience, captivated, sang along and waved their handkerchiefs, rapturous in their applause. Clearly touched by the warmth of his reception, Joe had a few words to say to those present in his characteristically blunt style: "I hope I was a little kind to Blackpool – but Blackpool was always bloody good to me."

There was a crisis involving Joe before the concert. He had arrived in Blackpool without proper sheet music for the songs he was to sing. Barry Morris, then Blackpool Council's Deputy Director of Tourism called on a favour from the BBC in Manchester and had Joe's rough notes transcribed into orchestra parts, a job that would normally have cost hundreds of pounds. Then, on the night of the concert, as the time for Joe's spot approached, he was nowhere to be found. In a panic Morris tracked him down to a nearby public house where he was enjoying a drink with Dr. Ken McGill, an old Blackpool friend from the 1950s, and shepherded him back to the theatre.

The headline in next day's Blackpool Evening Gazette summed up the audience's reaction to the evening in three short words: "It's Joe Show". They might just as well have called the Centenary Show 'The Josef Locke Show' and been done with it: "The swashbuckling Josef crowned the mammoth line-up… with his sheer showbiz talent and power." His powerful presence had "summoned [up] memories of an older Blackpool…a picture of the old-style Golden Mile…when Central Station was full of trains." The writer here put his finger on the secret of Joe's appeal. It was to an older generation remembering the 1940s and 1950s when the promenade and beaches were thronged with holidaymakers and the town was in its pomp.

Joe was back in Blackpool again in December to appear with Ken Dodd in the Centenary Christmas Show, which closed the year's celebrations in style. This was yet another charity event, when again Joe had his audiences singing along with him and loath to let him go. As it happened, however, he had only four further appearances in the resort in the following year, the first in March 1977 in a charity performance organized by his protégé Phil Kelly to fund a trip to Lourdes for Blackpool's handicapped children. The second was a 'top of the bill' appearance in an Easter Monday Spectacular at the Winter Gardens Pavilion in April. And finally there were two Sunday appearances at the South Pier on 24 and 31 July, before a dispute over payment between Joe and the promoters led to further performances being cancelled.

It would be another fifteen years before Joe was back singing in Blackpool, and then in circumstances which he could hardly have foreseen.

The Donegal Farm

The farm which Joe had bought outside the village of Burnfoot in County Donegal, a few miles over the border from Derry, was in a picturesque location, looking west on rolling slopes on one side of a valley. Soon after its purchase Joe set about building a large and comfortable modern bungalow for Carmel and himself, to which he gave the rather grand name of 'Drumellan House'. Its design took full advantage of its elevated situation, having a main lounge running half the length of the property, with large floor-to-ceiling windows along the western side giving wonderful views towards Lough Swilly. Ornately carved Victorian and Edwardian wooden furniture was brought up from Kilcoole along with Joe's cream-coloured baby grand piano (a gift from EMI, Joe's recording company in the 1950s). The new house was ideally suited for entertaining, and musicians and other friends from Derry visited Joe and Carmel there. Particularly welcome and longer-staying visitors were Joe's three children by Bertie Agnew.

By the mid-1970s Joe was reported as living on the Burnfoot farm in semi-retirement. He and Carmel had stables down the hill from the house and a number of brood mares from whom they hoped to get foals. They had a sheepdog Flossie, much admired for her herding abilities by the local farmers, but not, so far as one can discover, any sheep; and there were a couple of Doberman pinschers, guard dogs which only Joe could handle. Joe himself took an active part with Carmel in looking after the horses, seeing to their fodder, bringing them inside in the winter evenings and letting them out again in the morning. Maintaining them was a costly business and on one occasion, when four out of their six mares failed to become pregnant, Joe decided that they couldn't afford to keep them and sold them on.

However not all their time was taken up with farm work. Joe was a keen golfer and played regularly at the North West Club at Lisfannon outside Buncrana. Indeed in one letter to his son Karl he declared himself to be quite 'golfed out'. He and Carmel would also go to the Golf Club for bingo and have their lunch out. When Joe was away on his, by now infrequent, concerts around Ireland, Carmel generally stayed behind to look after the animals. The house was quite isolated, some way back from the road, and she must often have felt lonely and counted the days until his return.

The farm may not have been a paying proposition in any strict sense, but one can sympathize with Joe's exasperation and sense of grievance that the powers-that-be didn't appear to take his farming activities seriously, and treated the Burnfoot farm as a mere loss-making business venture designed to be set against Joe's income from other sources. "These people seem to think that because I sang occasionally at concerts and other engagements, I wasn't entitled to the normal grants available to farmers." Whereas, Joe insisted, "I told them that I was paying heavy tax on these show-business engagements."

It was presumably through working with animals on the farm that Joe got to know Paddy McGeady, a fellow Derry man and leading member of the Irish Veterinary Association, who arranged for him to entertain the delegates to the IVA's Annual Congress, when it was held in Bundoran early in October 1976. Maureen Hegarty remembers a hysterical drive back from Bundoran later that night. They somehow got lost taking a shortcut and were stopped by the Gardaí, with the car reeking from whiskey that had spilled from a bottle in Joe's hip-pocket. The back seat's all wet," Joe had joked, "I hope it's blood." To make matters worse, Joe had unfastened his trouser-belt for comfort and, as soon as he stepped out of the car, his trousers fell about his ankles.

Joe pictured in February 1975 with Derry soprano Maureen Hegarty, his sometime singing partner in the 1970s and 1980s. (By kind permission of Maureen Hegarty)

Other, more sober, local events he appeared at in the summer of 1976 were Derry's Civic Week, 29 May – 5 June (with Dana and Phil Coulter); Ramelton's Lennon Festival in July; the Letterkenny Folk Festival and a charity concert in the Fiesta Ballroom, Buncrana in aid of the Fahan Orphanage, both in August.

At this time Joe also became a regular guest on the local Radio Foyle station to sing a song or take part in a chat show. He also performed with local musicians in different shows around the North-West. Pianist Roy Adams recalls being asked by Joe to

accompany him in cabaret in Donegal. The piano had no music stand, but Joe said not to worry: he would hold the music for Adams while he played and Joe sang. However, 'within 6 bars of the opening' Joe, carried away on the wings of song, had laid the sheet music flat on top of the piano and was moving among the audience, leaving his poor accompanist to 'vamp' as best he could.

But then suddenly in summer 1977 Joe announced that he was putting the Burnfoot farm up for sale and was moving somewhere closer to Dublin. The reasons he gave were the already mentioned difficulty he was having in getting grants to develop the farm and a rekindling of his interest in performing in public. In Dublin he would be closer to the major venues, whereas in Donegal he was geographically speaking out on a limb. Their new home was another farm, near Edenderry on the border of Kildare and Offaly. As for Burnfoot, Joe may have sold or let out some of the farmland, but he held on to the bungalow which he continued to use off and on until 1983.

Edenderry

The house at Derrycorris on the outskirts of Edenderry was a very different property from the new-build Burnfoot bungalow. It was an old-world farmhouse complete with conservatory at the end of a long tree-lined lane. But although 'old-world', it was roomy and Joe had it renovated it and brought up to date with a fitted kitchen. Carmel loved it, more so perhaps than any of the other houses she lived in with Joe in the course of their nomadic life. It was surrounded by 30 acres of rich farmland and was bordered on the south side by the Grand Canal.

Initially the move south seemed to pay dividends. Joe had a two-week run early in June at the Olympia Theatre with Charles Lynch and Mary Sheridan in *An Evening of Music and Song*, followed later in the month by a week's run at the Cork Opera House. But the engagements gradually dried up or perhaps Joe's appetite for seeking them out waned.

Spanish Days

One reason for the infrequency of Joe's singing engagements at this period was that he was seldom in one place for long. Quite apart from his properties and his animals north and south of the border, he also owned a villa in Spain, where he took to spending long periods from the late-1970s onwards, usually over the winter months and around Easter. It was in Benalmádena Costa, south of Torremolinos, and had a gloriously central position a short walk from the sea.

In the early days he would drive Carmel and himself there, motoring down from Cherbourg in his green 5-cylinder Audi 100 LS. However by 1981, the 1600 mile drive was proving too much, and he asked his son Karl to hunt out an 'oul banger' in Madrid for him to use in Benalmádena. Joe loved the Spanish sunshine, warmth and lifestyle, and had been holidaying there from the early 1960s. He tanned easily, often returning to Ireland with a golden glow. An added attraction for him was that in Spain, unlike in Ireland, he was never recognized or pestered by fans. Carmel was less keen on Spain and fretted about their animals when she knew she was going away. To get around this, Joe would delay telling her they were going until the night before they were due to leave.

Between their holidays in Spain and other commitments at home, Joe was in effect semi-retired. In 1979, so far as one can discover, he gave no public concerts. And, although he topped the bill in Calum Kennedy's revival of the *Five-Past-Eight Show* in Glasgow's Theatre Royal for two weeks in September 1980, there was little else besides. In 1981 he was again without any singing engagements.

With one notable exception: on Sunday 4 October 1981 Joe and a number of other musicians (Phil Coulter, the folk group Clannad, Maureen Hegarty and Willie Loughlin) gathered together in Derry's Guildhall to celebrate James MacCafferty's fifty years as a musician. He was, of course, one of Joe's oldest friends and his accompanist in the 1969 Blackpool summer season. The show was informal, almost to the point of lacking structure altogether. Coulter, asked on the night to get the

Joe singing in front of the Guildhall organ at the October 1981 concert in Derry.

Gathered around the piano at the same concert are, from left: James MacCafferty, Phil Coulter, and Joe (second right). (By kind permission of Pat MacCafferty)

show up and running, was given no fixed running order. As a result, in the first half, MacCafferty's friends simply gathered around him at the piano and sang a few songs together. In the second half, compered by Don O'Doherty, Joe sang a duet with Willie Loughlin, and then another duet, 'Madam, Will You Walk?', memorably with Maureen Hegarty. She recalls how softly he sang to blend in with her lyric soprano voice, and also that she was eight-and-a-half months pregnant at the time and, in her own words, 'the size of a mountain'. It made the coy exchanges of the song so ludicrous that neither singers nor audience was able to keep a straight face.

Even Joe, 'the International Singing Star', was on this night just another musical son of the city. It was Derry looking at itself in a mirror and liking what it saw.

'The Mountainy Farmer'

It might have been being back in the north-west again and the welcome he received in his home town, or the absence of singing engagements elsewhere, but in January 1982, in a surprise move, Joe announced that he had bought Molloy's Bar in Burnfoot. It was just six miles from Derry and close to the house which he and Carmel still owned nearby. This purchase was the more surprising in that Joe's history in the licensed trade – from The Listowel Arms to the Ha'penny Inn and the Orchard Inn in Killincarrig

135

– had been chequered, to say the least, and it was only a few years earlier that he had professed himself to be glad he was no longer running a pub – giving as his reason, "that I couldn't put on a smile for the customers when I didn't want to."

For the remainder of 1982 and the following year Joe had no concerts. So, while keeping their home in Edenderry, Carmel and he moved north again, with Joe giving himself over full-time to making a success of his new venture. He changed the pub's name to The Mountainy Farmer – a fairly blatant, if implausible, reference to himself – and opened what had been a 'gentlemen only' bar to women – an innovation that may not have gone down well with the 'regulars'. It was said that among his occasional patrons was a judge whose presence in the pub was a safeguard against it being 'done' for after-hours drinking. It was also said that, despite his own past record in this regard, Joe didn't look kindly on patrons singing in his pub. Or perhaps it was just that he didn't like competition.

Among those who occasionally helped behind the bar was his son Karl, then a student at Queen's University in Belfast. He remembers his father providing him with a car and paying its running costs, but there was a snag – namely that, when Karl was coming over the border on his weekend visits, he should bring with him under wraps a few bottles of whiskey, which was cheaper in Northern Ireland than in the Republic.

Joe and His Children

Not all of Joe's dealings with his children involved bootlegging. In fact, although the public never got to hear of it, for all his failings as a husband, pre-Carmel, he seems to have been a fond, if not particularly demonstrative father. Yvette, his eldest daughter, remembers him in the 1950s having her to stay with him during the summer holidays when he was singing in Blackpool. Later, when the time came for her to choose a career he encouraged her to go in for the law and offered to support her in her studies. But when Yvette chose music as a career, Joe backed her up, often turning up in Belfast when, as happened annually in the 1980s, the RUC Ladies Choir, which she conducted, gave concerts in the Ulster Hall.[2]

Joe showed a similar interest in his children by Bertie Agnew. When their daughter Nikki was unhappy at her school in Belfast, he arranged for her to go to Loreto Convent boarding school in Bray and paid her fees. When Karl did well in his O-levels, he wrote to him in congratulation, and – perhaps conscious of his own curtailed schooling – urged him to see education as an asset. He continued to support him financially through university, although legally the requirement for him to pay maintenance ceased on Karl's 16th birthday. In his letters to the children as they were growing up he usually enclosed a five or ten pound note for them to spend on themselves. When his younger

---

[2] *At one of these concerts Joe's old friend Willie Loughlin was able to get his own back on Joe for calling him out of the audience at Morecambe some years before to perform onstage with him. Seeing Joe in the Gallery, Willie pointed him out to the Ulster Hall audience as 'a young man' – Joe was then in the 70s – who was anxious to sing along with him. Joe then joined Willie for an impromptu duet, followed it up with a couple of solos, and in the end could hardly be got off the stage.*

Two pages of a letter from Joe to his sons Karl and Peter in September 1976, when they were both schoolboys, stressing the importance of education. (By kind permission of the McLaughlin Family)

son Peter had helped deliver a foal at the farm in Burnfoot and Joe thought he might have talents in that direction, he offered to see him through veterinary school.

But it was not all about 'getting on'. As his children grew older, they came out to Joe's villa in Spain, first on their own, and later, when they were married and had families, with Joe's grandchildren. Welcome though this was, he sometimes joked about opening a 'B and B' and limiting 'family visiting' to 5 to 6 pm.

Only with Joseph, his first son, did Joe seem to struggle. His half-sister Nikki remembers him as a lovely child. An instance of this is a story from 1958 when Joseph was six years old and his father was in the Blackpool summer show with Ken Dodd. The comedian had constructed a web of fantasy about his 'Titterascope' – an earlier version of his famous Tickling Stick – a fictional device for getting the audience to laugh by tickling them with feathers concealed under their seats. During one performance an usherette found young Joseph scrabbling about under his seat. Asked what he was doing, Joseph said, "I'm looking for some of those feathers Ken Dodd's been talking about."

But there were indications, in his going missing as an eight-year-old and his later running away from home, that, with Joe and Betty warring over him, he was a troubled child. After Joe agreed to Joseph living with Betty in California, the loss of his son seemed to prey on his mind, although they continued to write to one another. It was a terrible blow to him, therefore, when he heard that Joseph had died quite unexpectedly in his twenties, a blow that those closest to him said he never fully recovered from.

Selling Up and Slowing Down

Then, in spring 1983, as suddenly as Joe had bought the pub, he put both it and the Donegal farm up for sale. Apparently he sold off the farm in small lots and – so the story goes – was paid in bags of cash rather than by cheque. The sale may have been forced on him for health reasons rather than from any loss of interest. A few months before he had been unwell and had undergone surgery, something he only revealed to his children some time later

This was Joe's first illness in many years and was a reminder that, as a 66 year old, he had neither the energy nor the stamina he once had. So, he and Carmel returned south to the Derrycorris Farm at Edenderry, leaving Donegal for good. Spain was next on their travels. They arrived in Benalmádena Costa in early May 1983, with Joe resolved to live there permanently, and to slow down to a pace befitting his age and health. Thus he did no public singing of any kind in 1983, and one could have been forgiven for thinking – as his wife Carmel no doubt did – that Joe had finally put his performing days behind him.

Braemor Rooms 1: The Comeback

It was a joke around Ireland that Joe had had as many final appearances as Frank Sinatra had had farewell tours. His first – involuntary – retirement had been back in

1958 when he had to leave England in a hurry to escape the taxman. He had talked of retiring in 1971 around the time of his marriage to Carmel. (And indeed businessman Pat Quinn, founder of the Quinnsworth supermarkets, was credited with coaxing him out of retirement in 1973 to sing at his sports hotel complex at Kilternan in South Dublin.). Joe had then announced he was retiring in April 1975 and that his concert with Peggy Dell on 29 April would be his last. And he had practically disappeared from public view in the years 1979 to 1983.

However at the beginning of February 1984, shortly before Joe's 67th birthday, it was trailed over the airwaves on a popular morning RTÉ radio show that he was to make a comeback. Within minutes the station switchboard was jammed with listeners phoning in, wanting to know 'where, when and how often'. And just before the show's end Pat Quinn – the same Pat Quinn mentioned above, who had probably planted the rumour in the first place – came on the line to say that Joe would be appearing under his promotion in a two-week cabaret run at the Braemor Rooms, part of the well-known entertainment complex 'The County Club', on Churchland Road, South Dublin.

Joe's first appearance at the Braemor Rooms on Monday 6 February 1984 put down a marker for the years that followed. Not that he didn't perform elsewhere. But the Braemor became for him from 1984 to 1991, in the final phase of his performing career, something almost like a residency, the venue he kept returning to, with the advantage of not being too far from his home in Edenderry. And there he formed a close musical liaison with a new singing partner, Rose Tynan. They had appeared together before – in a 'Sunday Night Special' in Cork Opera house in the summer of 1975 – but the Braemor shows marked the beginning of a regular collaboration between them, a variety double act which was to last for the best part of the next eight years. However, they were not a duo in the ordinary sense. Generally in their shows each stuck to his or her own well-tried solo repertoire of songs, only occasionally coming together in a duet.

Tynan, at this time aged fifty-two, was what would once have been described as a fine strapping woman, stout and generously proportioned, with tightly-curled short dark hair and a fondness for long dangly earrings and loose floating dresses. The eldest of ten children, she was brought up in humble circumstances in Moore Street in central Dublin where her family had a market stall, left school at fourteen and for a time earned a living sewing in a theatrical costumiers. Her breakthrough was in a 1950s Radio Éireann talent show when she was eighteen, and since then she had built up a reputation as a singer, initially of country and western songs; but by the time she and Joe were working together she was singing anything from Irish folk songs to jazz and rock and roll.

Joe's linking up with Rose Tynan, begun in the Braemor Rooms, was his first long-term professional partnership with a fellow singer since his time with May Devitt in the 1940s, and then he had been very much the junior of the two. With Rose he was clearly the lead singer and chief draw – and, it was said, insisted that he got the star's cubby-hole of a dressing-room at the Braemor, leaving her to make-up with the others. But as time went by, he increasingly grew to depend on her, relying on her to warm up the audience for his own spot later on in the show, and generally be his support.

After the February 1984 run in the Braemor Rooms Pat Quinn brought the same cabaret programme and artists to the Connolly Hall in Cork for two nights in March, followed by three nights in the Old Shieling Hotel in Raheny, North Dublin. In April Joe and Rose were back 'by popular request' for a week in the Braemor Rooms; and in May repeated their visit to the Old Shieling Hotel. They appeared together at the Rustic Inn in Abbeyshrule, Co. Longford, on two separate nights in July and August; and in between these appearances they were in *Josef Locke and Friends* in a week's run at Dublin's Olympia.

In fact, the only booking Joe had during this period in which Rose Tynan wasn't involved was on Saturday 14 April at the National Concert Hall when he appeared with the classical soprano Mary Sheridan and Brendan Grace.

The VATS award and *The Late Late Show*

The feeling was widespread in the early 1980s that Joe's career, if not definitively over, was drawing to a close. While his performances at the Braemor Room had shown there was still life in the old dog, there was a consensus that the time was ripe to celebrate his lifetime's achievement in show business. Hence the cluster of valedictory events centred on Joe in the closing months of 1984.

Early in October it was announced that Joe was to receive the Variety Artists' Trust Society's (VATS) annual award in recognition of his more than 40 years' contribution to the variety arts in Ireland. In fact, the citation credited him with '50 years' in the entertainment business, which would have him starting out in 1934 when he was in the Irish Guards. Previous winners of the award were Harry O'Donovan (1971), who with Jimmy O'Dea had helped launch Joe's career in the 1940s, Maureen Potter (1973) and Peggy Dell (1975), fellow performers with Joe in many shows down the years.

On Thursday 15 November, ten days before the award was due to be presented, the Lord Mayor of Dublin hosted a reception in Joe's honour in the Mansion House in Dawson Street. Joe turned up in a tweed suit and sporting the kind of Stetson cowboy hat worn by the character J.R. Ewing in the then popular TV series of *Dallas*. Joe spoke wistfully of his early days at the Gaiety Theatre with May Devitt, claimed – improbably, but perhaps he was overcome by the occasion – that he still loved singing opera best. He then put in a plug for the Olympia Theatre, where the presentation was to take place.

That was to be on Sunday 25 November. However the evening before, unflagged in advance and catching Joe unawares, he was the guest on a special one-and-a-half-hour edition of Gay Byrne's *Late Late Show* on RTÉ television devoted entirely to Joe and featuring his show-business colleagues, family and friends. That Joe hadn't known about the programme beforehand was clear from the look of disbelief on his face as Byrne led him on to the set. But he was soon at his ease, getting the show off to a rousing start with his familiar rendering of 'Blaze Away'. He then settled down with a pint of Guinness at his elbow, happy to oblige Byrne and the audience with reminiscences of his time as a choirboy in Derry, his early days with Jimmy O'Dea, and other stories from his gaudy past.

The show was punctuated by songs from Sonny Knowles, Sean Rooney and Rose Tynan – the latter in a duet 'Madam, Will you walk?' with Joe. Among others, Joe Lynch, Albert Healy and Michael McCarthy each had some cherished memory of Joe to recall to everyone's amusement. The studio audience, many of them old friends and colleagues like Vernon Hayden and Harry Bailey, were in a mood to celebrate Joe's life and make plain to him the warmth of their affection. Colleagues who had died, like Jimmy O'Dea and May Devitt, were fondly remembered.

The closing item on the programme was Joe singing Phil Coulter's song 'The Town I Loved So Well' about their home town, at that time still reeling from almost daily bombs and shootings of the Northern Ireland Troubles. Joe's voice, unsurprisingly, was not what it had been, but his ability to put a song across was as deft as ever, and here he pulled out all the stops, quickening and slackening the tempo to fit the mood of the words, at times swelling to a crescendo and at others dropping down to pianissimo, almost speaking the lines rather than singing them. In its own way it was a tour de force, and drew a storm of applause from the audience, not least from Derry's MP John Hume who could be seen involuntarily beating time with his left hand as Joe came to the closing lines:

"I can only pray for a bright brand new day
In the town I love so well".

The public saw a side of Joe on *The Late Late Show* that they perhaps wouldn't otherwise have directly experienced – the spontaneous and easy charm, the gift of the gab and the joshing exchanges with friends and colleagues. Of course, they already knew him as a singer from the theatre and the concert hall, and over the years Joe had developed a good rapport with an audience and a jokey line in patter. But the format of the television chat show allowed him over the ninety minutes to be more natural and reflective, without having to project himself as a 'star' or celebrity. And they might have caught at the show's end something they couldn't easily have seen from the stalls or the balcony: Joe with the hint of a tear in his eye.

The following evening the VATS award was presented to Joe at a star-studded 'Gala Concert' in Dublin's Olympia. The theatre was packed was twelve hundred people present; another six hundred were turned away. The Lord Mayor of Dublin, the Mayor of Derry and many guests from *The Late Late Show* were there to see a glittering variety cast delight the audience and pay their tributes to the toast of the evening, among them veterans of the theatre like Noel Purcell, and younger performers like Rose Tynan. Joe was delighted with the turn-out, commenting on the audience's response: "They simply won't let me retire." It was the last time that Joe would appear at the Olympia, but it was not by any means his swan-song.

The portrait by Pat Phelan presented to Joe on Gay Byrne's Late Late Show on Saturday 25 November 1984. (By kind permission of the McLaughlin Family)

Braemor Rooms 2

In the years from 1985 to 1991 Joe appeared in cabaret at the Braemor Rooms on no less than sixteen separate occasions, usually, though not invariably, with Rose Tynan as his support act. The only year when this wasn't the case was 1986 when he had to go into the Blackrock Clinic in Dublin for major heart surgery and spent the second half of the year recovering. Other than the Braemor Rooms his public performances were now almost without exception limited to one-night stands, even in places like Cork where he would once have played for a week to packed houses.

There remains a testament to Joe and Rose's time at the Braemor Rooms in a 1985 live recording of selections from their cabaret show, issued as *The Songs I Love So Well* on the Irish Harmac label. It features many of Joe's old favourites – 'Blaze Away', 'The Old Bog Road', 'Slievenamon', 'I'll Take you Home Again Kathleen', 'Goodbye' and 'Danny Boy' – together with newer songs – 'On the Street where you Live' and 'My Way'. There was also a duet between Joe and Rose, Offenbach's 'The Bold Gendarmes'; one of only two instances of a duet in Joe's recordings.

Astonishingly, even at this late date Joe seems to have toyed with the idea of another overseas tour. There was talk in summer 1988 of going to Australia; and in September of that year a Canadian newspaper carried an advertisement in which he was billed to appear at the National Arts Centre in Ottawa with comedian Gene Fitzpatrick. But it was not to be: belatedly his place was taken by another, younger Irish tenor, Frank Patterson.

Among the occasional charity events and festivals around Ireland in which Joe appeared in the later 1980s it is worth mentioning two in particular, as they show his career coming round full circle. The power and quality of Joe's voice had first been recognized when he was training RUC recruits in Enniskillen. He had not been back there to sing since 1946. But now in the twilight of his career he revisited the town – the first time on Friday October 1988 when he appeared at the Ardhowen Theatre overlooking Lough Erne and received a standing ovation. He returned the following summer as part of the 'Enniskillen Festival' with Maureen Hegarty, John Cooke and The Derek Marsden Trio, to be greeted like a long-lost son – 'Enniskillen's own international singing star' – and was given the whole second half of the show "to regale the audience with his greatest hits."

Joe was not to know that in the audience that night were two young men who had a particular interest in his performance. Together, they were to bring Joe back into the public eye in a way he had not known since his heyday in the 1950s.

CHAPTER TEN

The Last Goodbye
1991-1999

Letting Go

In 1991 aged 74 Joe finally called it a day on his performing career. He made a few final appearances in cabaret with Rose Tynan at the Braemor Rooms between May and September that year. Shortly afterwards the club closed its doors for the last time, to reopen as a different sort of nightclub, 'Faces' with a different and younger clientele. In other ways, too, Joe was closing his accounts. In June he put his Edenderry farm up for auction and announced to the press that Carmel and he were moving to Spain and meant to live there permanently.[1] It was one of Joe's typically off-the-cuff remarks and he may not have consulted Carmel beforehand. Although Joe loved Spain, they were never to settle there permanently but they did continue to visit the Joe's villa there from time to time, sometimes for months on end. Instead they spent most of their time in 'Sorrento', a pleasant modern bungalow in Clane, County Kildare a few miles from Carmel's childhood home in Celbridge.

There on sunny afternoons, when Carmel was working in her garden, Joe would sit down at the piano and, with the windows open, sing for her 'I Hear you Calling Me'. On other days he would make his way to Jones' pub in the town's Main Street and settle down in one of the snugs with a pint of Guinness to do the crossword in the *Irish Times*. And so, perhaps, Joe's life might have drifted to its conclusion, but for the general release in 1992 of the feature film *Hear My Song* that brought the ageing star of a thousand variety shows back into the public eye, led to fresh invitations to appear in shows in England the United States, and sent CDs of his old recordings soaring in the pop charts.

Hear My Song

The film was the brainchild of film-maker Peter Chelsom, who had listened to a tape of Joe's songs on a long motorway drive. Impressed by what he had heard, Chelsom brought up Joe's name with Barry Morris, Blackpool Council's then Director of

---

[1] *Joe had clearly been intending to sell the farm at Edenderry for some time, as he had sold off all the farm livestock in January 1989. Fortunately for Joe, this was just a few days before the canal that bordered the farm was breached and flooded the land.*

Joe photographed in relaxed mode in his later years.

Tourism, who told him the story of Joe's seasons in Blackpool and about his notorious flight from the Inland Revenue. Chelsom saw immediately that it had the makings of a screenplay and set about adapting Joe's story for the cinema with the help of Irish actor Adrian Dunbar as co-writer.

By a strange coincidence, Chelsom's parents had had an antique shop in Blackpool called The Golden Age which Joe frequently visited in the 1950s when he was living locally, and his characteristic autograph had pride of place in their Guest Book. Dunbar, who was from Enniskillen, was too young to remember Joe singing there in the later 1930s, although his parents and older relatives might well have recalled hearing a 'Constable Joseph McLoughlin' in St. Michael's Church or at the Foresters' Hall.

Learning that Joe was to appear at the Ardhowen Theatre in Enniskillen on Saturday 19 August 1989, Chelsom and Dunbar turned up for the performance and sought him out after the show that same evening. At the time their script was only half-written and the whole project struck Joe as half-baked. "Bloody mad" were his words to them. But the two young writers weren't put off and over the following months the script gradually took shape.

The story of the film, while it sticks to the bare facts of Joe's brushes with the taxman and the warrant for his arrest, romanticizes them in a number of ways. Dunbar was cast as Micky O'Neill, a young English club manager and general wheeler-dealer, whose girlfriend's mother (played by Shirley Anne Field) had been a beauty queen 'Miss Dairy Goodness' a quarter of a century previously, and had had an affair with Josef Locke just before he fled back to Ireland. Initially Micky tries to save his struggling club by booking a 'Mr. X' who looks and sings like Josef Locke, but is exposed as a fraud when he clumsily attempts to seduce the former beauty queen. Micky realizes that there is nothing for it but to go over to Ireland, seek out the reclusive Josef Locke, and talk him into coming back and singing at his club. Only by getting Locke to agree will Micky reverse the club's fortunes and recover his place in his girlfriend's affections.

That's the basic story-line; and, although it takes all kinds of liberties with Joe's

Cathleen (Shirley Anne Field) and Jo Locke (Ned Beatty) in the 1991 film Hear My Song.

actual history – for, as we know, Joe carried on with his singing career quite openly all the time he was in Ireland and also settled with the Inland Revenue after nine years – it works very well as a romantic comedy; and by the film's end only the most flinty-hearted wouldn't rejoice in Joe and his friends putting one over on the policeman (David McCallum) who is hunting him down.

When Chelsom and Dunbar went back to Joe with a draft completed script, his initial scepticism had given way to a wary acquiescence that the film should go ahead, subject to certain conditions: the principal one being that Chelsom agree not to touch on the spicier aspects of Joe's life and career.

The other important decision concerned the casting of the Josef Locke character. Buncrana-born Ray McAnally had been Chelsom's original choice for the part, but he died suddenly of a heart-attack in June 1989. As his replacement Chelsom plumped for American actor Ned Beatty whom he thought had the proper charisma, combined with the necessary facial resemblance to Joe. Joe himself at first queried the choice of Beatty, citing the actor's lack of height as his main objection, and then, perhaps less seriously, complaining that Beatty was not as good-looking as he was. However it seems that he eventually warmed to Beatty's portrayal, grudgingly admitting that the American – dubbed with Vernon Midgely's singing voice – had done a good job.

There was a late crisis when the filming was about to start. Joe, having decided to be as good as his word about retiring, had gone off to Spain with Carmel and left Ireland without signing off the clearance rights to the film. Chelsom had to fly out to find him and eventually tracked him down in a Spanish bar, tanned and relaxed, and totally oblivious to the need for his signature.

Filming on Set

Filming started in October 1990 and took seven and a half weeks. The main shoots were in Dublin, County Clare and the Wicklow Hills. The former Plymouth Brethren's Merrion Hall at the corner of Merrion Square in Dublin was temporarily fitted out with an art deco bar and a false proscenium arch to be the theatre in which 'Jo' (the shorter name used in the film) was to perform. While filming was going on in Dublin, film director Alan Parker was also in the city filming *The Commitments*, a musical tale of a very different sort about a Dublin rock group, and it seems that the film extras occasionally got confused as to which film set they were meant to be on, with ludicrous results. Otherwise everything went smoothly, and Chelsom as director seems to have gone out of his way to ensure that everyone involved in making the film had a good time. William Hootkins, who played 'Mr. X', later said that it was "the only movie I've done which [was] one long continuous party from the first casting session to the premiere."

News that the film was shortly to be released galvanised a number of journalists to go looking for Joe in Clane to obtain an interview. In this case the real-life Joe proved as elusive as the Jo in the film, sometimes denying point-blank that he was the quarry they were seeking, at other times putting them off with bland or flippant replies to their questions. Asked about his former escapades, he was careful not to say anything that would embarrass Carmel or cause her distress. As for his past reputation as a man for the ladies, his joking response was "In my position as a star, I'd have been an eejit if I wasn't." But he wouldn't be drawn to elaborate further.

The film had a few screenings in advance of its official London premiere. One of the first was at the Claddagh Place Cinema in Galway on Saturday 20 July 1991, where it closed the Galway Arts Festival. There were further screenings in Enniskillen in a charity event organized by the local branch of the Round Table, and at a Film Festival in Derry in November. It was also shown in Los Angeles on Thursday 23 January 1992, after which Madonna rose to her feet and led a standing ovation. She said she had thoroughly enjoyed the movie, although the music was not quite her sort of thing. There were even reports that the film was being tipped for an Oscar.

Singing for the Princess

The London premiere was on 3 March 1992 in the Odeon Cinema at Marble Arch, and was attended by Princess Diana. The event was in aid of 'Turning Point', the charity for the homeless of which Diana was Patron. Joe and Carmel were flown over to London for the occasion, with Joe making a wry joke about the cost of Carmel's designer gown. He himself wore a black evening suit with his, by then, thinning grey hair skirting the collar of his jacket.

Given that the film was about Joe, he was understandably, along with the Princess, the centre of attention. When Chelsom introduced him to the audience at the film's end, they rose to applaud him. He then sang 'Danny Boy', before being introduced to the Princess, of whom he claimed to be a great fan. It had been, he said, almost exactly forty years – November 1952 – since he had last sung before 'a Royal'.

In the midst of all this, a surprise was sprung on him when Michael Aspel, host of the TV show *This is Your Life*, appeared from behind a curtain and announced to the audience that Joe was to be subject of the next programme. Mouth agape at the news Joe was promptly whisked away to record the show at London's Teddington Studios. It was broadcast eight days later, on 11 March. In the studio were several who had performed with Joe during his long career, notably Will Fyffe Jnr who had accompanied him on piano when he had sung at the Royal Variety Performance in 1952. Joe's family were there too: his wife Carmel, his eldest daughter Yvette, and younger children Nikki and Peter. It was Carmel, in league with others in the McLaughlin family (chiefly his younger brother Brendan), who had provided the inside-knowledge that gave the show its appeal. For that purpose, unknown to Joe, they had gathered together old photos and memorabilia from his past.

Meanwhile, back at London's Cumberland Hotel, the post-premiere party had started in Joe's absence, but didn't come to life properly until he arrived back from the television studios. Joe began to sing and went on singing, all the time promising that his next song would be his last – 'a strategy', the watching press commented 'that ensured the crowd would be begging for more.' Those in the know said it was just like the filming: the songs, the drinking and the craic. Joe serenaded Shirley Anne Field with the song 'She Moved through the Fair' and, gallant as always, remarked that he would "jump at the chance at a liaison with such a fine-looking lady." But, meeting 'the stoney gaze of his wife' (the press's words), he quickly backtracked, saying that of course he "no longer went in for that sort of thing."

Dublin and Blackpool Premieres

The Dublin premiere followed on 5 March at the Savoy Cinema in O'Connell Street. Joe, 'resplendent in a Kelly green checked sports jacket and tinted glasses', cut a dandified figure. He lovingly – and, it was said, 'obligingly' – kissed Carmel on the lips for the benefit of the waiting crowd and gaggle of pressmen and photographers. The next day the *Irish Press*, noting the age and sex of many of those in the crowd, headlined its report, 'Lovely Old Ladies Go Wild for Josef'.

At the after-show soiree in the nearby Gresham Hotel, Joe again sang 'She Moved through the Fair'. The director, script-writers and cast then joined Joe's family for dinner and drinks. Alcohol flowed freely, but when one of the younger Northern Irish actors showed signs of being the worse for drink, Joe asked him to leave, saying he didn't want him making a spectacle of himself in front of the family. The celebrations then shifted to the Gaiety Theatre, continuing into the wee small hours. Finally, the week ended with Joe making a guest appearance on Gay Byrne's *Late Late Show*. For a man in his mid-seventies this was a tiring schedule.

The Blackpool premiere followed a week later on 12 March in the Cannon Cinema, on the site of the former Hippodrome where Joe had sung so often. The 700-strong audience, including show-business figures like comedians Les Dawson and Roy Walker, gave Joe a standing ovation as he walked along a specially designed catwalk decorated with his initials. After the film, there was complete stillness as he gave, yet again, a 'faultless unaccompanied' performance of 'She Moved through the Fair'. He had, the press said, the audience 'in the palm of his hand'. Then another party, this time in Blackpool's Imperial Hotel, which went on well into the night, with Lancashire Hotpot washed down with champagne, and more singing.

Shortly after, the film went on general release throughout Britain and America, picking up a number of nominations and awards, among them a BAFTA award for the Best Screenplay and a British Comedy Award for the Best Film. There was talk of Joe being invited to give a concert in New York's Carnegie Hall or, closer to home, at The Point in Dublin's Docklands (now the 3Arena), but Carmel worried that it would be too much for him and persuaded him to turn the offers down. In truth, Joe must have realized that his voice was past its best and that his reputation was better served by people listening to recordings he had made decades earlier.

Press coverage in Blackpool of the premiere of the Hear My Song film in March 1992. (Evening Gazette, 13 March 1992)

Climbing the Charts

Following the appearance of the film around the country, record companies such as EMI saw an opportunity to cash in on the publicity generated by the film by re-issuing recordings of songs from Joe's back catalogue. These had originally appeared on 78 rpm records between 1947 and 1957. Now released as tapes and CDs, these recordings grabbed the attention of a new and younger audience: the children, or indeed grandchildren, of those who had bought them in Joe's heyday. With the result that Joe, at the age of 75, became the oldest performer ever to reach the Top Ten album chart, his recordings sitting incongruously alongside those of Madonna, Simply Red and Queen.

On 8 April 1992 Joe's *Hear my Song* collection reached No. 9 in the Pop Album Charts, earning him an EMI Silver Disc. Two days later, Joe was out and about in Dublin city centre signing copies of the CD for members of the public. (Joe's recording career stretched from 78rpm records, to 45 rpm discs, through to LPs and cassette tapes, and then, in later life, to CDs. But he always referred to CDs disparagingly as 'those wee things'). He started off with a walkabout in Moore Street, a market area jam-packed with stalls and shoppers. There he sang for 'Peggy', one of the stall-holders and a lifelong fan, and rattled off a few one-liners. Then he made his way to the HMV store on Henry Street, according to the press, like 'the Pied Piper with followers in his wake'. He sang there as well. A few days later, sales of *Hear My Song* passed the 100,000 mark, earning him a Golden Disc to go with his Silver one.

Signings and walkabouts were one thing, singing in a concert or show was another. He did, however, appear at a few charity functions in the following months. In June he was at Clontarf Castle to celebrate the career of Maureen Potter, his one-time colleague with Jimmy O'Dea at the Gaiety. Three months later he put in an appearance at a charity event in the Westbury Hotel in Dublin to launch a special 'audio-described video' of Chelsom's film for blind/partially sighted people. In September he also took part for the last time in a special edition of Gay Byrne's *Late Late Show* to mark the programme's 30th anniversary. He may have been persuaded to appear by the fact that two of the guests on the programme were (again) Maureen Potter and another old friend of Joe's from Listowel, the playwright John B.

Joe photographed with playwright and pub-owner J B Keane. The two became friends during Joe's summers in Ballybunion and Listowel in the later 1950s.

Keane – the other guest being the former Taoiseach Charlie Haughey.[2] Joe sang the Frank Sinatra number 'My Way' which over the years had come to sum up for him, as for Sinatra, the light and the dark places in his long and varied life.

He was not in good voice and one reviewer next day caustically referred to his 'caterwauling', which may have stung Joe if he read it. But in any case he must have realized that his singing days were behind him.

However, he was to have one last time in the spotlight, and it came with an invitation to appear at the Royal Variety Performance in London in December 1992.

The Royal 'Goodbye'

It took place in London's Dominion Theatre in the presence of the Prince and Princess of Wales, one of the last times they were to appear together before their separation. Joe was not originally scheduled to appear in the show. The list of names of the artists performing was printed in the programme and Joe's was not among them. One must assume that, because of the publicity surrounding Chelsom's film and the unexpected success of Joe's CDs in the charts, it was decided to include him at the last minute.

This was not the barn-storming figure of his prime, but an old man taking his final leave of the public. As he went on stage he spoke quietly into the microphone, "I'm finished…but it's not bad to finish on a Royal Variety Performance," and sang just the one song, his usual signature closing number, 'Goodbye' from *The White Horse Inn*.

In the end it was not about how well he sang. The voice was thin where it had once been full-bodied, he had difficulty keeping in time with the orchestra, and the closing high notes were beyond him. But it was an opportunity for the audience to show their affection for the old trouper and thank him for the pleasure he had given down the years, and this they duly did. Then, with a bow to the Royal Box and a final guardsman's salute, he left the stage for the last time.

The Final Curtain

This time there was no coming back. He lived out his final years quietly with Carmel, mainly in their bungalow in Clane, their visits to Spain becoming rarer as Joe's health declined. But there were occasional visits to England and Northern Ireland to see Joe's children and grandchildren.

In Clane Joe was still to be seen in Jones' pub in the afternoons with a pint of Guinness mulling over the *Irish Times* crossword. He enjoyed the occasional cigar but didn't smoke cigarettes unless they were a Spanish brand that he had taken a liking to and which he got his son Karl, a linguist, to bring over from Spain. The locals for the most part left him alone, although it seems he could sometimes be persuaded to sing when he had a drink or two inside him.

---

[2] *There is a story that when Haughey was Minister of Finance in the Irish Government in the later 1960s he bought land in the city centre from Joe which he subsequently re-sold at an enormous profit. If true, it would be one of the few occasions when Joe was bested financially by a fellow-Irishman.*

In his later years Joe listened to a lot of music on the radio. According to Carmel he liked most kinds of music except jazz. Richard Tauber was a particular favourite, but he had time for the younger Irish tenors like Anthony Kearns and Ronan Tynan. He would tune in to Val Joyce's music shows on RTÉ, both his nightly *Late Show* and his Saturday afternoon show that combined both Joyce's (and Joe's) twin passions, for music and horse-racing.

His acceptance of retirement was perhaps linked to a growing sense of his own mortality and increasing frailty. He had lost a number of his contemporaries, old friends and colleagues, in the early 1990s. Vernon Hayden, who had first shown him how to apply make-up and was with him on the New Zealand-Australia tour of 1961, died in 1990; bandleader Mike Delahunty collapsed and died in February 1992, shortly after his band's farewell appearance; and Cecil Nash, a singer in Joe's Olympia shows, died in 1993. Joe himself was becoming more and more infirm, a shadow of his former self. The cream-coloured baby grand piano, which had held pride of place in Joe's various homes since the 1950s and on which he would play for Carmel, was heard less often now. A burglary at the bungalow in the mid-1990s unsettled him, forcing him to add more locks to the house.

Summer 1996 and spring 1997 saw two significant celebrations for Joe and Carmel: their 25th wedding anniversary in August 1996 and Joe's 80th birthday eight months later. Both occasions were spent quietly: the first celebrated at home with close family; and then, on Joe's birthday, he and Carmel had dinner together at the nearby 'K Club'. Otherwise they seldom went out. As Joe's health deteriorated Carmel had to become as much his nurse as his wife. Even with outside help this was difficult. Joe had lost a lot of weight, but he was still a big man and, when he fell over, he couldn't easily be got up again. Nevertheless Carmel cared for him at home during his last two years when he was an invalid and it was only when this became impossible, two weeks before the end, that she faced up to the inevitable and agreed to him going into a nearby private hospital on Prosperous Road.

Joe died on Friday 15 October 1999. He was eighty-two years old, and the world of entertainment mourned the loss of one of its brightest stars.

The Requiem Mass took place in St Patrick's and St Brigid's Church in Clane, directly opposite Jones' pub, on Monday 18 October, on a mild, but sunny autumn day. The small church was filled with over 300 mourners: family, friends, fellow entertainers and townspeople. Mary Sheridan and Rose Tynan were there, and, standing out from the other mourners, Captain Michael Tiernan, the Taoiseach's aide-de-camp, in his full braided uniform – a public acknowledgement by the State of all that Joe had meant to his fellow-countrymen and women. Carmel, Joe's widow, was accompanied by Joe's five surviving children.

In his homily the priest talked about 'Joe the family man', a side of his life Joe had kept hidden from public view. Family members had brought to the church some mementos of the husband, father and grandfather they had loved: his favourite tie, book of crosswords, and the Gold Disc from EMI of which he was so proud. There were, too, moving words from Carmel read out at the service by Joe's son Karl, in which she recalled how Joe had played the piano and sung for her. She said she knew the angels would now be playing their harps for him. Those in the congregation who knew Joe well would have smiled to themselves at this, thinking that the angels might also be wondering, once Joe started singing, would he ever stop? Joe's eldest daughter Yvette, her voice choking with emotion sang 'The Lord's Prayer'. Then, towards the end of the mass, tenor Anthony Kearns sang 'Ave Maria' and 'I Hear You Calling Me', the very songs Joe himself had sung at his debut concert in Enniskillen in 1939.

The townspeople of Clane stood in silence as Joe's two sons, Karl and Peter, helped carry his coffin out of the church. Later that day the funeral cortege made its way to Dublin en route to Glasnevin Crematorium, leaving behind Kildare with its stud farms and pasturelands where Joe had spent so many happy years, both in his prime and in his retirement. His ashes were placed in an urn in Glasnevin Cemetery in Dublin under a grey slab. The simple inscription reads: 'Joseph McLaughlin 1917-1999', with 'Josef Locke' written in brackets underneath.

Ireland's Taoiseach Bertie Ahern, speaking from an EU summit in Finland, expressed his sadness at the news of the singer's death. There were many tributes to Joe in newspapers across Ireland and Great Britain. In America the *New York Times* ran a headline, 'Irish Tenor Who Inspired Tears Is Dead', crystallizing in a phrase the effect of Joe's voice on so many people who had heard him sing over the years. Nobel Laureate Seamus Heaney described him as 'the man with the song in his heart'. But it was a comment by fellow Derry man, Phil Coulter which best summed up what many who came to know Joe felt about him: "The world is full of grey people…Joe was multicoloured."

We'll leave the last words to Joe himself. When it was put to him in 1992 that he had had a wonderful life, he replied: "Why wouldn't I? A big fine fella like me?"

A big fine fella indeed. And what a fine voice too.

Outline Chronology of Josef Locke's Life

1917	Born 23 March at 19 Creggan Street, Derry-Londonderry.
1924-30	Sang as boy treble in St Eugene's Cathedral Choir, Derry
1934	Enlisted in the Irish Guards; based in England
1936-38	Served with the Irish Guards in Egypt and Palestine
1939	Joined the Royal Ulster Constabulary as Constable 5349
	1st documented public concert in Foresters' Hall, Enniskillen
1940	Transferred to Lisburn RUC Barracks
1941	Married 1st wife, Esther (Essie) McKeown in Lisburn, Co. Antrim
	Moved to Leopold Street RUC Barracks, Belfast
	Resigned from the Police Force, after Belfast audition with Jimmy O'Dea
	1st Variety Show tour in Ireland as a professional entertainer
	1st Dublin appearance in the *So What* revue at the Gaiety Theatre; met May Devitt
	1st documented Belfast appearance in *Come to the Show* at the Empire Theatre
1942	Birth of 1st child, daughter Yvette
	1st public concert in his hometown Derry, at the Guildhall
	1st (and only known) oratorio performance, tenor solo in Handel's *Messiah*
1943	1st radio broadcast, on the BBC For the Forces wavelength
	Left his 1st wife, Essie McKeown
1944	Operatic debut in *Madame Butterfly* in Dublin's Gaiety Theatre
	1st (and only known) lead role in a musical: *Showboat* at Dublin's Gaiety Theatre
	1st pantomime role, in *Puss in Boots* in Cork Opera House
1945	1st London appearance in *Salute to Variety* show at the Victoria Palace
	1st appearance in Blackpool, a one week run at the Palace Theatre
1946	1st full Blackpool season in *Starry Way* revue, alongside George Formby
	Divorce *nisi* from 1st wife, Essie in Belfast High Court
1947	Married 2nd wife, Doreen McMartin in Sacred Heart Church, Durham
	2nd full Blackpool season in *Ev'ry Time You Laugh* revue
	Release of 1st record (78rpm) with Columbia Label: 'Sorrento' and 'Santa Lucia'
	Birth of 2nd child, daughter Moira
1948	1st film *Holidays with Pay* with Mancunian Films
	3rd full Blackpool season in the *Coconut Grove* revue
1949	1st appearance at the London Palladium in a 3-week run
	2nd film, *Somewhere in Politics*
	1st appearance at the Royal Albert Hall, replacing Tito Gobbi
	Birth of 3rd child, daughter Violetta (Leta) by Doreen McMartin
	4th full Blackpool season in *Coconut Grove* alongside Julie Andrews
	1st television appearance on BBC's *Rooftop Rendezvous*
	3rd and final film with Mancunian Films, *What a Carry-On*
1950	Death of new-born 4th child, an unnamed daughter
	JR Wyrill Heyworth concert series began
	5th full Blackpool season in *Sunny Serenade* revue
	Death of 2nd child, Moira from whooping cough
1951	6th full Blackpool season in *Moulin Rouge* revue, 1st time as business partner
	Marriage to 2nd wife, Doreen McMartin declared null and void
1952	Married 3rd wife, Betty Barr in Marylebone Registry Office in London
	1st overseas tour to Canada with Tommy Trinder
	1st Royal Variety Performance in the London Palladium
	Birth of 5th child, and 1st son, Joseph by Betty Barr

Chronology

1953	7th full Blackpool season in *Singing in the Reign* at Queen's Theatre
1954	1st American trip, visited Las Vegas, New York, Hollywood
1955	1st Dublin appearance in 10 years at the Theatre Royal
	2nd and 3rd American trips, and separation from 3rd wife, Betty
1956	4th American trip, including concert in New York's Carnegie Hall
1957	Met new partner Roberta (Bertie) Agnew
1958	8th full Blackpool season, in *Let's Have Fun* on Central Pier
	'Flight' from Blackpool and warrant issued for his arrest
1959	Birth of 6th child and 5th daughter, Nikki, by Bertie Agnew
1960	Birth of 7th child and 2nd son, Karl
1961	Bought the Listowel Arms Hotel, renamed it The White Horse Inn
	Bought the Corn Exchange on Dublin's Burgh Quay with business partner
	Tour of New Zealand and Australia with other Irish artistes
1962	Birth of 8th child and 3rd son, Peter
1963	Bought The Ha'Penny Inn pub on Dublin's Wellington Quay
1965	3rd wife, Betty given custody of son Joseph
1966	Final separation from Bertie Agnew
1967	Bertie Agnew awarded damages against Joe in assault case in Dublin High Court
	Return to Blackpool Bankruptcy Court and settlement of tax arrears
	Sentenced to 4 months' imprisonment for removing documents from Dublin Castle
1968	9th full Blackpool season in *The Queen's Show* at the Queen's Theatre
	Won appeal against imprisonment; £50 fine imposed instead
1969	10th and final, full Blackpool season at the Queen's Theatre
1971	Canadian trip to record 4 television programmes
	Married 4th wife, Carmel Dignam in Chesterfield Registry Office
1972	Concert in Dublin's National Stadium for 'Bloody Sunday' families and internees
	11-concert 'Bogside Tour' in Derry and Donegal
1975	Retirement Concert at Dublin's RDS; now living in County Donegal
1976	Centenary Command Performance at Blackpool Opera House
1979	Bought the Derrycorris farm in Edenderry, County Offaly
1980	Last 2-week run in variety in Glasgow's Theatre Royal
1982	Bought Molloy's Pub in Burnfoot, Co. Donegal; renamed it The Mountainy Farmer
1984	Comeback in cabaret shows at Dublin's Braemor Rooms with Rose Tynan
	90-minute television tribute in Gay Byrne's *The Late Late Show* on RTÉ
	Presentation of the Variety Artists' Trust Award in Dublin's Olympia Theatre
1986	Major heart surgery at Blackrock Clinic, Dublin
1989	Approached by *Hear My Song* script-writers at Enniskillen's Ardhowen Theatre
1991	Last appearance at Dublin's Braemor Rooms
1992	London, Dublin and Blackpool premieres of the *Hear My Song* film
	Award of EMI Gold Disc awarded for sale of re-issued recordings
	Final public appearance at his 2nd Royal Variety Performance; sang 'Goodbye'
1996	Celebration of Silver Wedding (25th) Anniversary with 4th wife, Carmel
1999	15 October, died in a private hospital in Clane, County Kildare, Ireland

Epilogue

Josef Locke wasn't somebody who kept in regular touch with all the people in his life. He could turn up without warning at a theatre, pub, race or golf course, to be greeted warmly by people he hadn't seen in years, and then as quickly disappear. But what of the people – the friends, the family and fellow entertainers – who were central to Joe's life over its eighty-plus years?

At the end of her singing career **May Devitt** spent her retirement between the homes of her grown-up children in Toronto, Dublin and South Africa. She stayed in touch with Joe, sending him the occasional postcard. May died from a heart attack on 13 April 1977 while staying with a married daughter in Cape Town.

Rose Tynan, Joe's singing partner in cabaret, died in September 2001, almost exactly ten years after Joe's last appearance with her at the Braemor Rooms.

Joe and his first wife **Essie** remained close friends throughout their lives. She remarried, coincidentally to another policeman. Joe's eldest daughter Yvette – herself a fine singer – spent her working life teaching music and conducting choirs, She was awarded the MBE for services to music and the community in 2011.

Doreen McMartin, Joe's second wife, remained in Lancashire for the rest of her life. It is said that she never fully recovered from the death of her two infant daughters, and she never remarried. Doreen died in March 1992, and Joe is said to have wept at the news. Their sole surviving daughter, Leta (Violetta) attended her father's funeral in October 1999. She still lives in Lancashire. In later life **Bertie Agnew** married an ex-Merchant Seaman, with whom she lived in Belfast until her death in 2012. Her children with Joe: Nikki, Karl and Peter live in England and Spain.

Many of Joe's show business colleagues pre-deceased him. Comedian **Danny Cummins**, Joe's long-standing co-star at the Gaiety, was killed in a road accident in December 1984, aged seventy. Shortly before he died, he arranged that, as his coffin passed from view at Glasnevin Crematorium, Joe's recording of 'Blaze Away' would be played. It was Cummins' last joke. **Erik Ellison** ('Mr X') continued to perform his Josef Locke impersonation until his death in November 2008, aged 90. By then, he too had acquired his own impersonators.

The Ha'penny Inn on Dublin's Wellington Quay was repossessed after Joe's failure to repay his loan on the business. It currently belongs to Tipperary-man Mick Ryan, who has photos of Joe on display in his pub. In Joe's home town of Derry a bronze memorial to him, designed by Terry Quigley, was unveiled outside the City Hotel by Phil Coulter and John Hume on 22 March 2005.

Carmel McLaughlin, Joe's widow, lives quietly in County Kildare. She is devoted to his memory.

There are many people of Irish extraction around the world for whom Joe's singing of Irish songs and ballads continues to have a strong emotional appeal. One such lady, who had lived her entire life in Glasgow, was so moved by Joe's singing of 'Galway Bay' that she asked for her ashes to be scattered there. She had never been to Ireland, but Joe's singing represented for her the Ireland of her dreams and imagination.

Index

Productions and Touring Shows

Venues